Sandinista Communism and Rural Nicaragua

THE WASHINGTON PAPERS

. . . intended to meet the need for an authoritative, yet prompt, public appraisal of the major developments in world affairs.

President, CSIS: David M. Abshire

Series Editor: Walter Laqueur

Director of Publications: Nancy B. Eddy

Managing Editor: Donna R. Spitler

MANUSCRIPT SUBMISSION

The Washington Papers and Praeger Publishers welcome inquiries concerning manuscript submissions. Please include with your inquiry a curriculum vitae, synopsis, table of contents, and estimated manuscript length. Manuscripts must be between 120–200 double-spaced typed pages. All submissions will be peer reviewed. Submissions to *The Washington Papers* should be sent to *The Washington Papers*; The Center for Strategic and International Studies; 1800 K Street NW; Suite 400; Washington, DC 20006. Book proposals should be sent to Praeger Publishers; One Madison Avenue; New York NY 10010.

The Washington Papers/143

Sandinista Communism and Rural Nicaragua

Janusz Bugajski

Foreword by Mark Falcoff

Published with The Center for
Strategic and International Studies
Washington, D.C.

PRAEGER

New York
Westport, Connecticut
London

Library of Congress Cataloging-in-Publication Data

Bugajski, Janusz, 1954–
    Sandinista communism and rural Nicaragua / Janusz Bugajski ;
foreword by Mark Falcoff.
        p.   cm. – (The Washington papers, ISSN 0278-937X ; 143)
    "Published with the Center for Strategic and International
Studies, Washington, D.C."
    ISBN 0-275-93535-3 (alk. paper). – ISBN 0-275-93536-1 (pbk.)
    1. Frente Sandinista de Liberación Nacional. 2. Nicaragua –
Politics and government – 1979- 3. Minorities – Nicaragua – Political
activity. 4. Communism – Nicaragua. I. Title. II. Series.
JL1619.A52B84   1990   89-71093
335.43'097284 – dc20

The *Washington Papers* are written under the auspices of The Center
for Strategic and International Studies (CSIS) and published
with CSIS by Praeger Publishers. The views expressed in these papers
are those of the authors and not necessarily those of the Center.

Library of Congress Catalog Card Number: 89-71093
ISBN: 0-275-93535-3 (cloth)
       0-275-93536-1 (paper)

First published in 1990

Praeger Publishers, One Madison Avenue, New York, NY 10010
A division of Greenwood Press, Inc.

Printed in the United States of America

∞

The paper used in this book complies with the Permanent
Paper Standard issued by the National Information Standards
Organization (Z39.48-1984).

10 9 8 7 6 5 4 3 2 1

Contents

Foreword

Few revolutions in the Third World have evoked so much passion in Western countries as the Sandinista assumption of power in Nicaragua. No doubt this has been largely due to the role of the United States in the Central American conflict, especially the war of bullets and words between Managua and Washington. It is also true, however, that the new regime in Nicaragua arouses worldwide interest and sympathy because it claims to represent a new synthesis of social reform and revolutionary power – much as the Soviet Union, China, Cuba, or Vietnam did in the past. Paradoxically, the death of socialism in Eastern Europe and even possibly the Soviet Union has only accelerated the need for alternatives, and *Sandinismo* consciously positions itself to benefit from the disillusionment with earlier models of revolutionary change.

The message is often repeated – sometimes by people who by no stretch of the imagination could be regarded as sympathetic to the Sandinista government – that there is something different about the revolution in Nicaragua. As far as official rhetoric is concerned, the program of *Sandinismo* ("pluralism, a mixed economy, a nonaligned foreign policy") seems closer to Scandinavian social democracy than to communism, and 10 years into the regime, the degree of economic and political pluralism in Nicaragua far exceeds that of Castro's Cuba at an equivalent point in time. What is this society, and where is it headed?

One good way to find out is to look closely at Nicaragua's most crucial economic sector – agriculture – as Janusz Bugajski has done in his remarkable monograph. He studies not merely where Nicaragua is today, but which patterns for the future can be discerned from ongoing policies. Through the careful, systematic peeling away of layers of rhetoric and euphemism, he shows that in the countryside (where most Nicaraguans live) the Sandinistas have constructed an economic system driven wholly by ruthless political imperatives. The results have been a catastrophic decline in productivity on the one hand and a festering of political dissent on the other. The civil war that has been raging in the northern provinces and on the Atlantic Coast since 1982 or 1983 has fed upon these frustrations, and nothing – including tactical concessions by the Sandinistas – seems to have fully reconciled the differences between the government's vision of the future and its needs for short-term political peace.

Nor are these differences likely to be reconciled. One of the particular contributions of this monograph is to show how the government has managed to hold firm to its essentially Leninist vision while resorting to unfamiliar expedients; it has circumvented the explosive issue of land ownership and sought to regiment the peasantry through other forms of pressure – taxation, price policy, input allocations, and a monopoly on the purchasing and distribution of foodstuffs. These apparently technical matters have become burning political issues, and until they are frankly acknowledged as such and dealt with accordingly, they will remain to undermine the country's civic peace and its economic health. Meanwhile, Janusz Bugajski provides an exceptionally valuable guide to a complicated and often confusing issue, with implications that far transcend Nicaragua or Central America.

Mark Falcoff
Resident Scholar
American Enterprise Institute
for Public Policy Research

November 1989

About the Author

Janusz Bugajski is a fellow in East European Studies at the Center for Strategic and International Studies. During 1984 and 1985, he was a senior research analyst at Radio Free Europe in Munich, West Germany, and earlier served as a consultant and researcher on Polish affairs for BBC Television in London, England.

Born in Cheshire, England in 1954, Bugajski obtained a B.A. (Honours) from the University of Kent at Canterbury, England (1977), and an M.Phil. in social anthropology from the London School of Economics and Political Science (1981).

Bugajski's books include *Czechoslovakia: Charter 77's Decade of Dissent* (1987) and *East European Fault Lines: Dissent, Opposition, and Social Activism* (1989). He is currently writing a book on *Fourth World Conflicts: Communist Policies, Rural Societies, and Indigenous Peoples*. He was a contributing author to *Soviet/East European Survey* in 1985, 1986, and 1987, and a regular writer on current events in Eastern Europe for *Radio Free Europe Situation Reports* and *Background Reports* in Munich during 1984 and 1985.

Bugajski's articles have appeared in several international periodicals and journals, including *Problems of Communism, The Washington Quarterly, Political Communication and Persuasion, Encounter, The National Interest, The New Republic,* and *The World and I.* He has also conducted freelance research for the Rand Corporation in California and has lectured at Georgetown University, Johns Hopkins University, Duke University, the Smithsonian Institution, and the Foreign Service Institute, Department of State.

Acknowledgments

I especially thank the Lynde and Harry Bradley Foundation for their generous support for this project. This paper on Nicaragua is part of a wider study of Communist policies toward rural populations and indigenous peoples that will be completed in 1990.

Research material for this paper was obtained from the Library of Congress, the Georgetown University Library, the Indian Law Resource Center, and several other libraries and institutions in the United States and Europe.

Invaluable research help was provided by Heidi Liszka, Jean Carlo Rivera, Carolyn Winn, Alison Hoffman, Alina Zyszkowski, Dorothy Tomaszewski, Tamara O'Seep, Ellen Stroud, Maria Bucur, Jasmine Kosovic, Christina Jordan, Kevin Callinan, Stefan Sullivan, Edward Horgan, Peter Gajda, and especially by Olga Petrovich, who accompanied me on a productive fact-finding tour of Central America.

Summary

When the Sandinistas seized power in July 1979, they embarked on a "socialist transformation" of Nicaraguan society. In confronting major internal and external obstacles, however, the Sandinista regime opted for some economic flexibility without abandoning its longer-term political objectives. The regime's Leninist political arrangements were therefore combined with a quasi-Communist economic program. The Sandinistas captured and remodeled all levers of social control, including the state apparatus, the armed forces, and the security network, and fortified those mechanisms that could most effectively extend Sandinista domination. But to uphold productivity, obtain vital agro-export revenues, prevent international isolation, and minimize economic dislocation, political opposition, and social unrest, Managua implemented a transitional "mixed economy" and continued to tolerate a politically emasculated private sector.

In evaluating the impact of Sandinista political, economic, and social programs, this study focuses principally on the confrontations between the regime and Nicaragua's rural population, particularly the *ladino* peasantry and the Indian and black indigenous minorities of the Atlantic Coast region. It concentrates on the Sandinistas' agrarian strategies to distinguish between short-term policies and long-term programs. And it addresses the question as to whether any durable and novel ideological, political, and economic elements have been introduced in Nicaragua, especially vis-à-vis the peasantry and the country's ethnic minorities.

By maintaining control politically, militarily, and economically, the Sandinistas will retain the option of accelerating the pace of political Leninization and economic socialization if they consider domestic conditions conducive and international pressures surmountable. Because Nicaragua has no institutionalized checks on the powers wielded by a partisan political force, policies can be altered without legalistic constraints. Sandinista rule is not circumscribed by genuine political competition, nor does it depend on a popular mandate to support its major policy decisions. In such a situation, almost all reforms, concessions, and compromises with capitalists, peasants, ethnic minorities, and other social groups are ultimately tenuous and reversible. Nicaragua's agrarian population and its indigenous societies will therefore continue to be subject to Managua's tactical twists and strategic turns.

Sandinista
Communism
and Rural
Nicaragua

Introduction: A Brief Overview of Marxism-Leninism

The first successful Communist takeover on the American mainland occurred in July 1979, when the Sandinista National Liberation Front (*Frente Sandinista de Liberación Nacional* or FSLN) seized power in Nicaragua. Subsequent Sandinista domestic policies provide a valuable laboratory and a largely accessible case study of how a Marxist-Leninist system is imposed and adapted in a developing country.

In assessing the FSLN's objectives, achievements, and setbacks in its planned "transition to socialism," this study will focus primarily on the confrontations between the Sandinista regime and Nicaragua's rural population, particularly the *ladino* or *mestizo* (mixed Caucasian and Amerindian) peasantry and the Indian and black indigenous minorities of the Atlantic Coast region. To understand the principles and operations of newly formed Leninist regimes in Third World nations requires an examination of the political, social, and economic impact of government policies on the rural sector. In developing states such as Nicaragua, agrarian capitalists, peasant proprietors, and landless farm workers often form a majority of the economically active population, and their output is usually crucial for both domestic consumption and foreign export earnings. Even though Nicaragua's ethnic minorities constitute a small percentage of the populace, they inhabit a region spanning almost half the national territory. Moreover, their resistance to Sandinista rule has proved persistent and resilient and provided a major focus of international criticism against Managua's policies.

Since seizing power, the FSLN has partially camouflaged its attempts to lay the foundations of a Communist system, or it has implemented changes gradually and incrementally to avoid international ostracism and isolation, to prevent the emergence of a unified and effective internal opposition, and to minimize the costly social and economic dislocations normally associated with the consolidation of one-party rule. Despite this gradualist approach, the Sandinistas have painstakingly laid the framework of a Leninist state and the groundwork for a "noncapitalist" development strategy in both urban and rural areas of Nicaragua during the past decade. This volume will analyze the Sandinistas' agrarian strategies to distinguish between the regime's short-term policies and its long-term programs. It will also address whether, in terms of Marxist-Leninist models of state socialism outlined in the introduction, any durable and novel ideological, political, and economic elements have been introduced in Nicaragua, especially vis-à-vis the peasantry and the country's ethnic minorities.

Marxism-Leninism is an all-embracing political doctrine containing principles that purportedly explain the entire course of human history. It also provides justifications and prescriptions for conducting revolutions to transform societies into "socialist formations." Through their analysis of late feudalism and early capitalism, Karl Marx and Friedrich Engels claimed to have discovered the "materialist laws of history" applicable to all socioeconomic structures. Their theories were subsequently simplified and solidified into a political dogma and a prophetic interpretation of social change. Practitioners of Marxism such as V. I. Lenin revised the original theory by setting the "subjective factor" of Communist Party policy above the "objective conditions" of socioeconomic development as the chief agent of revolution. Since the Bolshevik takeover in Russia, Leninist Marxism has been applied by national Communist movements, including the Nicaraguan Sandinistas, to serve the interests of the revolutionary leadership. It consists of a diagnosis of world history, an agenda containing specific political and economic objectives, and a flexible timetable and methodology for attaining them.

The Marxist view of social evolution was anchored in the periodization of historical development, analyses of specific modes of production, and prognoses for revolutionary change between these modes.[1] Marx constructed a schema outlining the evolution of society to demonstrate his historical materialist conception that social life is formed by the structure of production. He visualized four basic stages of development, corresponding to specific social divisions of labor and to various forms of property – the tribal-communal, slave owning, feudal, and capitalist – culminating in the establishment of socialism. Social revolutions were viewed as the maturation of class struggles present in every form of society, propelling each society toward a new mode of production.[2]

Although Marx did not propose a rigidly predictable process of unilinear succession, his analytical stages were subsequently adopted by Marxists as a universal model of historical progress. Engels systematized Marx's ideas about social evolution and formalized their determinist and materialist elements.[3] "Historical materialism" became an all-encompassing doctrine with a unilinear view of social development in which supposedly superior socioeconomic systems necessarily replaced inferior ones.[4] The writings of Marx and Engels achieved canonical status for Communists; any variations on the basic evolutionist and materialist themes simply served to justify different applications of the doctrine in divergent local settings. Practical political considerations shaped Marxism (or "scientific socialism") into a coherent doctrine, providing the emerging Communist movement with a relatively simple and effective ideological tool.[5]

Lenin's revision of orthodox Marxism consisted of increasing emphasis on organized revolutionaries to accelerate the historical process and hasten the advent of socialism. In Bolshevik estimations, socialism did not emerge spontaneously but as a result of systematic preparation by the "Communist vanguard." Lenin constructed a powerful, hierarchically organized "party of a new type" to restructure society by imposing a "proletarian dictatorship," abolishing private property, suppressing all rival political groups, and imposing central control over all significant facets of public life. Socialism was to be constructed through planned economic development under close Communist Party supervision. Soviet leaders believed that dictatorial methods would be necessary to eradicate resistance in the countryside and to force the pace of capital accumulation and industrialization. The agricultural "surplus product" was to be appropriated by the state through the forced requisitioning of crops and the eventual collectivization of the peasantry under party tutelage. Some respite was introduced under the New Economic Policy of the early 1920s to stimulate private agricultural production and avert economic disaster.

After Lenin's death, Joseph Stalin relaunched and completed rural collectivization, which had disastrous consequences for the peasantry but ensured full state control over the agrarian population.[6] Stalin further rigidified Marxism in the 1930s to vindicate his policies.[7] The "doomed" social strata, including the patriarchal, tribal, feudal, and peasant populations, were considered historical remnants without any future under socialism. The mission of the party was to "abolish the old relations of production" forcibly during the revolutionary transition.

After failing to generate proletarian uprisings in capitalist Europe, Lenin developed his theories of imperialism. These theories rationalized the increasing attention of Soviet policy toward promoting revolutions in "colonial and backward" states and gaining non-European allies against the capitalist powers.[8] Lenin calculated that colonial wars and national liberation movements were the most important strategic reserve for the international Communist movement against "international imperialism." The masses of Asia, Africa, and Latin America could apparently bypass capitalism or interrupt it at an early stage in pursuit of "noncapitalist development" en route to socialism.[9] The Soviet regime was destined to play a crucial role in fomenting such socialist revolutions outside Europe.[10]

Marxism-Leninism became an ideological tool both for the seizure of power and for rapid noncapitalist industrialization in developing countries. The Soviet system became a pertinent model for Communist parties seeking power and eager to embark on "historical progress." The original Marxist prerequisites for socialist revolution, including the full development of capitalist "productive forces" and a large, organized proletariat, were either diluted or discarded by Third World Communist movements. Leninist theory and praxis served as an apparent quick fix to domestic retardation. Its appeal rested on the portrayal of economically polarized societies, whether or not these visions approximated Marx's class categories.[11] Communist parties were believed to possess the correct answers for eradicating poverty, class divisions, and national antagonisms, while propelling their respective societies toward the socialist millennium. The Marxist schema of social evolution was modified to suit local conditions, and its general premises were manipulated to legitimize state policy. Following the Soviet example, industrialization and proletarianization became a consequence and not a cause of socialist revolutions.

Lenin stressed that because of insufficient capitalist development in Third World states, local Communist parties had to exploit nationalism in their struggle with imperialism. He also pointed out the importance of the local bourgeoisie and peasantry as a potentially revolutionary force.[12] Communists had to forge temporary alliances with "patriotic" capitalists in colonial countries, but needed to avoid amalgamation and uphold the autonomy of the revolutionary "proletarian movement." These propositions were developed by Stalin and his successors in their multifarious "united front" approaches for seizing power, in which the Communist Party had to assume control of the "national liberation" struggle to throw off the "imperialist yoke." Hence, temporary compromises and alliances with the "national bourgeoisie" and other political groups were permissible as long as they did not obstruct the party's socialist objectives. Leninist organizations in the Third World have also excelled in appropriating nationalist and populist currents and in disguising their long-term objectives.[13] Numerous anti-Western and nationalist demands have been exploited and internal conflicts or aspirations manipulated to the party's advantage.

Communists believe they are endowed with a historic mission in largely agricultural or "backward" countries to accelerate socioeconomic development along a "noncapitalist" road.[14] Several key ideological and political goals that Leninists pursue toward rural populations and indigenous ethnic minorities will be explored here as they apply to Nicaragua. After a successful takeover, the party embarks on a program of reorganizing the countryside on a "socialist basis." Although there is no single, rigid schedule for socialization, as various domestic and international factors enter the equation, several important ingredients of this "revolutionary transformation" can be mapped out.

In dealing with "precapitalist" societies, Communist regimes aim for "detribalization," signifying the eradication of traditional systems of community, authority, and subsistence. An equivalent process of "depeasantization" is pursued among the "feudalist" or "capitalist" agricultural population. The party combines a combative ideological explanation about the retrograde nature of "tribalism" and "agrarianism" with a purportedly historic mission of forging national integration and a new "class consciousness." Communists attack tribal and peasant autonomy as "regressive conservatism" and seek to eliminate all vestiges of rural self-reliance. This may also involve state-enforced population transfers and the settlement of nomadic or dispersed groups in controllable territorial units.

To elicit public support or acquiescence, the party may underscore its commitment to cultural and religious freedoms, agrarian reforms, social justice, political pluralism, and other popular causes. Once the organization is more firmly entrenched, however, a new set of policies gains prominence. To eliminate sources of opposition while remolding society according to doctrinal specifications, Communists emphasize strict political centralization. This centralization involves the imposition of party-state controls over all important public institutions and activities. New political structures and social organizations are created for this purpose, with a vast bureaucratic expansion and the recruitment of politically reliable cadres. The administrative apparatus places severe restrictions on political and civil liberties and builds an intricate web of social controls.

In its economic agenda, the party appropriates the major means of production and launches a program of agrarian socialization. The state nationalizes all major industries, financial institutions, raw materials, transport, and communications and embarks on centralized economic planning. The wholesale elimination of the private sector can be delayed or even indefinitely postponed, but its unrestrained expansion and political impact are strictly curtailed. Communist regimes may tolerate some capitalist operations on the assumption that premature haste may cause unnecessary economic damage. Independent producers may coexist with the growing state sector as long as the latter controls the "commanding heights" and the former serves state interests through its high productivity. The farmers' "surplus" is exploited for urban industrial development through compulsory procurement and high taxation, while state control over the domestic and external market ensures central direction over economic processes.[15]

Communists view collectivized agriculture as a higher form of socioeconomic organization, facilitating state planning and enhancing the transition to socialism. Cooperative farming has therefore often been promoted despite its glaring inefficiencies. Collective farms are not simply economic units but political institutions of local government, social control, mass indoctrination, and social mobilization. They are the purported prototypes of a future "communist society" in which the "virtues of collective life" are instilled in the rural population.

Once the essential levers of Communist political, economic, and social control are firmly in place, various kinds of reorganization and reform may be undertaken to boost production. Indeed, partial decollectivization and the stimulation of private enterprise through various incentive schemes in some states have led to a significant growth in agricultural output. It is useful to distinguish, however, between temporary retreats from full-scale socialization designed to arrest serious economic decline and efforts at ostensibly permanent rural reprivatization. Nonetheless, even in the latter scenario the political changes accompanying agrarian reform have been circumscribed to prevent the reemergence of a strong "capitalist class" or of organized peasant opposition. The instruments of economic control may be loosened during a process of reform, but the party's political monopoly is maintained. Moreover, even the most reform-minded Leninist governments envisage the completion of "agricultural socialization" at a higher level of mechanization once economic modernization has been attained and the "means of production" sufficiently developed. The ideological goal of Communist regimes is the creation of a homogenous rural and urban proletariat and the emergence of a "classless" society.

Leninist parties in various parts of the world, however, are now facing increasing internal pressures to reassess some of the methods employed in attaining these exalted objectives. In stemming economic decline and avoiding falling further behind the capitalist states, a growing number of ruling parties have decided to backtrack from some of their socialist programs while maintaining their political controls and upholding their most essential long-term goals.

In assessing the application of Marxism-Leninism to

Nicaraguan conditions, this volume's first chapter provides a condensed history of the Sandinistas until their successful takeover of state power. Among the issues considered are the FSLN's self-serving alliance strategies, propaganda deceptions, and political maneuvers. In the realm of ideology, the chapter describes Sandinista attempts to blend Marxism-Leninism with radical Christian "liberation theology," anti-Americanism, Nicaraguan nationalism, and socioeconomic reformism. These ploys were designed to broaden the public reach and popular appeal of the Sandinista movement.

The second chapter outlines the levers of political and social control imposed and wielded by the FSLN since 1979 that have had a considerable impact on both rural and urban residents. These control mechanisms have been principally geared toward the following objectives: neutralizing or eliminating the political opposition; centralizing all branches of the state apparatus under Sandinista hegemony; constructing a Leninist-type vanguard party; extending and consolidating the regime's control over all major coercive instruments, social institutions, and mass organizations; and establishing a transitory "mixed economy" focused on "noncapitalist development" en route to a planned "socialist mode of production."

The third chapter begins with an overview of Nicaragua's complex agrarian structure and the position of the peasantry. It then presents a more detailed evaluation of the objectives, programs, strategies, and tactics adopted by the Sandinistas toward the agrarian populace – including the large, medium, and small farmers, the land-owning and land-renting *campesinos* (peasants), the landless laborers, and the agricultural wage workers. The following issues are specifically addressed: nationalization and centralization; mass mobilization and militarization; political indoctrination and Leninization; land reform, expropriation, and redistribution; and the pursuit of socialization and collectivization. This chapter also examines the daunting agrarian problems faced by the FSLN and the policy adjustments it has made in trying to reconcile ideological and political objectives with less than ideal economic and international conditions.

The fourth chapter focuses on Nicaragua's small indigenous Indian and Creole populations inhabiting the Atlantic Coast region. It traces the ideological elements underlying the Sandinistas' ethnic policies and evaluates the key government measures in its program of consolidating central control, promoting "national integration," and implementing far-ranging economic and social changes. Also discussed are the obstacles faced by the regime in the East Coast region and the concessions it has made to pacify the population while ensuring overall compliance with its directives.

The fifth and final chapter considers the significance of the Sandinista-contra civil war for the *ladino* peasantry and the country's native peoples. It measures the military involvement of indigenous and peasant populations in the internal conflict, as well as the political, economic, and social implications of insurgency and counterinsurgency operations for Managua's long-term programs of agrarian development and socialization. The role outside actors play in Nicaraguan affairs is also touched upon, especially the import of current Soviet and U.S. policies for a newly established "socialist-oriented" state such as Nicaragua.

1

Sandinismo: History and Ideology

Like many other Latin American countries, Nicaragua had a tradition of authoritarian political culture and a stratified class structure that obstructed the full emergence and development of a capitalist liberal democracy. The roots of instability can be traced back to 1927, when the Somoza family assumed power after a century of civil warfare and U.S. intervention in support of either Liberal or Conservative Party protagonists. The Nicaraguan National Guard was created as a professional nonpartisan army to maintain public order.[1]

When Anastasio Somoza Garcia became commander, however, he turned the guard into a virtual private army to consolidate his power and eliminate political opponents. The ruling Liberal Party was transformed into a dictatorial political machine, and Somoza assumed the presidency. The Somoza dynasty alienated an assortment of social classes and political groups, including much of the business community and the country's labor unions. Although overall living standards gradually improved in the country, inequalities between rich and poor widened; for example, more than 50 percent of the rural population lived at or below the subsistence level. Despite the fact that national economic performance improved under the Somoza family dictatorship from 1927 to 1979, the mass of the population remained politically disenfranchised, materially impoverished, and subject to repression if they lodged protests against domestic conditions. The third and last Somoza dictator, Anastasio Tachito, proved to be politically inept compared with his predecessors, who had successfully divided, co-opted, and controlled the major opposition groups. To capture state power, the Sandinistas exploited oppressive conditions and government illegitimacy during the popular insurrection in the late 1970s.[2]

Leninism in Nicaragua can be traced to 1944 with the establishment of the pro-Moscow Nicaraguan Socialist Party (*Partido Socialista Nicaragüense* or PSN). The PSN organized openly until 1950, when it was officially banned and its leaders driven underground or into exile. Although it continued to operate, its membership rarely exceeded 200 people. As did other Latin American Marxist-Leninist parties at the time, the PSN rejected violence because it considered "objective conditions" insufficiently ripe for revolution. Carlos Fonseca, a cofounder of the FSLN and its leading ideologue, was active in the PSN's student wing during the 1950s. Fonseca and his comrades became increasingly disillusioned with the inflexible and ineffectual PSN; Fidel Castro's takeover in Cuba in 1959 accentuated their frustrations.[3] Fonseca visited Havana and was encouraged by Castro and Ernesto "Che" Guevara to organize a Fidelista-type movement in Nicaragua. An initial attempt to spark a revolt and seize power in 1959 proved a disaster and Fonseca fled to Cuba, where several Sandinistas subsequently received much of their military and political training.

The Founding of the FSLN

At a meeting in Tegucigalpa, Honduras in 1961, Fonseca, Tomas Borge, and Silvio Mayorga established the National Liberation Front (*Frente de Liberación Nacional* or FLN).[4]

The Sandinista label was added in 1962 at Fonseca's insistence; it provided a veneer of nationalist legitimacy and the appearance of continuity with the campaign of Augusto Cesar Sandino against U.S. influence in the 1920s and 1930s.[5] From the outset, the FSLN was controlled by an elitist group of Marxist intellectuals with direct ties to the Cuban regime. In their political mythology the new organization initiated the "irreversible progress" of the Nicaraguan revolution through the creation of a "revolutionary vanguard."

Throughout the 1960s, the FSLN remained a minuscule force of about 100 combatants confined to the northern border areas. Because it failed to ignite any popular insurrection, its campaigns consisted largely of bank robberies and the assassination of local officials. Unable to gain sufficient backing among the peasantry and agrarian laborers, the guerrillas failed to establish a secure rural base.

The FSLN's version of Fidel Castro's *focista* strategy, in which a small core of revolutionaries aimed to seize power swiftly by igniting mass insurrection and a governmental collapse, proved unrealistic following major defeats at the Rio Coco in 1963 and at Pancasan in 1967. A new program was therefore developed. Its proponents were known as members of the Prolonged Popular War (*Guerra Popular Prolongada* or GPP), because they espoused a protracted "people's war" modeled on the Chinese and Vietnamese experience. A mobile guerrilla force was to conduct mobilizational work among the peasantry, build a formidable military and political structure, and gradually expand the Communist-controlled "liberated zones." In 1969 the FSLN formed a National Directorate (*Dirección Nacional* or DN), with Fonseca as general secretary to coordinate its operations (figure 1).

The GPP strategy proved disappointing, however, as few peasants rallied to the Sandinista cause, and most remained indifferent to its political message. No durable "liberated zones" were created, and by 1976 the FSLN's small "peasant base" was destroyed by government forces. Fonse-

FIGURE 1
The History of FSLN Development, 1961–1979

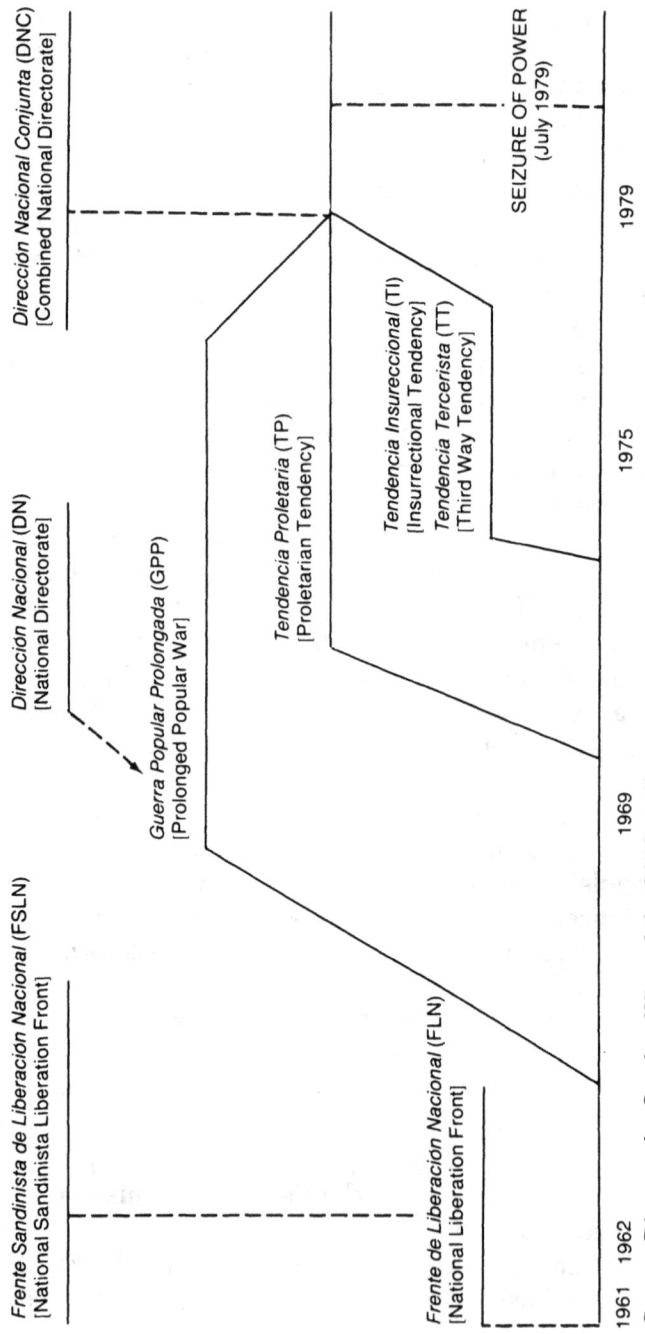

Frente Sandinista de Liberación Nacional (FSLN)
[National Sandinista Liberation Front]

Dirección Nacional (DN)
[National Directorate]

Dirección Nacional Conjunta (DNC)
[Combined National Directorate]

Guerra Popular Prolongada (GPP)
[Prolonged Popular War]

Tendencia Proletaria (TP)
[Proletarian Tendency]

Tendencia Insurreccional (TI)
[Insurrectional Tendency]

Tendencia Tercerista (TT)
[Third Way Tendency]

Frente de Liberación Nacional (FLN)
[National Liberation Front]

SEIZURE OF POWER
(July 1979)

1961 1962   1969   1975   1979

Source: Diagram by Carolyn Winn of the CSIS staff.

14

ca was killed, Borge captured, and the guerrilla remnants
withdrew into the eastern coast jungles. By 1970 the *Frente*
numbered about 70 full-time members and several hundred
clandestine supporters.[6]
   During the next crucial decade the organization survived various factional conflicts, launched a number of successful assaults on government targets, and steadily increased its membership. In the late 1970s, a new faction of
the FSLN, the Insurrectional Tendency (*Tendencia Insurec-
cional* or TI) or Third Way Tendency (*Tendencia Tercerista*
or TT) gained prominence. The two other major factions,
the GPP and the Proletarian Tendency (*Tendencia Proletaria* or TP), lost influence for their inability to gain any substantial measure of political or military control in the country or to launch the Communists into power. The GPP failed
to build a mass peasant-based movement, while the TP,
which stressed the creation of a proletarian-based organization, proved unable to motivate the urban work force.
   The TI differed from the other two factions primarily
on questions of strategy and timetable rather than ultimate
goals. Unlike the GPP and TP, which opted for a protracted
"consolidation of forces" and patient organizational work,
the TI believed that the time was ripening for a nationwide
uprising in the late 1970s. The *terceristas* emphasized the
creation of beneficial alliances with other anti-Somoza
forces and a mass insurrection in both city and country at
an opportune moment. The TI's stress on insurrection, con-
venient "class alliances," and a more gradual "socialist transformation" *after* the capture of power was criticized by other factions and more traditional Communists as "ideological
deviations." The *terceristas* opposed the TP policy of building a workers' party before the insurrection, fearful that
this would delay or block military opportunities. In their
estimation the "objective conditions" for socialism could
best be constructed, and the "revolutionary consciousness"
of the working class instilled, after the FSLN takeover. Indeed, the TI tended to dismiss revolutionary prospects
among Nicaragua's proletariat and peasantry and concentrated instead on the "third force" of disgruntled urban

youth, university students, marginalized *lumpenproletariat*, and "petit bourgeois elements." By May 1977 the *terceristas* dominated the DN and adopted a new FSLN political-military platform calling for a "popular revolution" led by the FSLN vanguard and a gradual transition to socialism, given the country's inauspicious economic, social, and geostrategic conditions.

By March 1979 the three Sandinista factions were formally unified in a nine-man Combined National Directorate (*Dirección Nacional Conjunta* or DNC) with three representatives (*comandantes de la revolución*) from each tendency. The much publicized "unification" was designed to create an impression of broad and diverse political forces coalescing. In fact all non-Marxists were excluded from key leadership positions, although differences within the DNC were "more a matter of partial and temporary disagreement concerning political analysis and military strategy rather than a real struggle for power."[7]

Castro played an important role in the unification process and in devising future FSLN strategies. *Frente* unity and an end to factionalism were the preconditions for consistent Cuban military and political support. Castro reportedly also advised Sandinista leaders to display tactical moderation with a slower pace of economic socialization following the takeover in comparison with the Cuban experience.

The "objective conditions" for insurrection had evidently matured by the late 1970s. They included a highly repressive dictatorship, a lack of governmental legitimacy, and Somoza's inability to accommodate growing aspirations among various sectors of society. Growing government corruption and ineptitude bred opposition and increasing international isolation. Popular outrage and opposition to Somoza mounted after the January 1978 assassination of Pedro Chamorro Cardenal, a highly respected independent publisher.

The FSLN was initially caught unprepared for the largely spontaneous local revolts, but as armed clashes increased, the guerrillas sought to direct the insurrection.

Their chief source of support was among unemployed urban youth, radicalized students, and some plantation workers, while peasant backing remained very restricted. The Sandinistas were the only sizable organization with a military arm that stepped into the growing power vacuum to coordinate the rebellion.[8] Somoza played into FSLN hands by delaying his resignation and thereby preventing a peaceful transfer of power to a coalition government. This lessened the potential impact of the democratic opposition, intensified the civil war, and enhanced the role of the *Frente*. About 5,000 FSLN irregulars launched the "final offensive" in March 1979 and seized power in July.

Sandinista ideologists portrayed their triumph as a process of "national liberation" in which the proletariat played a subsidiary role vis-à-vis the "middle sectors of towns and cities."[9] The Communist victory was described as a "democratic-popular revolution" by the "third social force" of semi-proletarians, students, *barrio* youths, and the petite bourgeoisie under the FSLN's "vanguard leadership."[10] This "popular democratic phase" was a means for "consolidating the revolution" and gradually "organizing the masses for socialism, a historically concrete mode of production."[11]

Because the Sandinistas possessed neither a large and reliable mass base nor an entrenched and powerful organizational structure, their alliances with disaffected sectors of society proved essential. Although the FSLN's application of Castroism had finally borne fruit, major differences with the Cuban model of revolution soon became evident. They revolved around the continuing post-takeover alliances with "bourgeois elements" and the concomitant slower pace of "socialist construction."

Sandinismo as Ideology

Sandinismo as a publicly proclaimed ideology is a flexible mixture of nationalist, populist, and reformist themes manipulated to serve the political interests of the FSLN's

Marxist-Leninist leadership.[12] The various components of *Sandinismo* have been tactically underplayed or emphasized to mobilize public support, to preserve pluralistic appearances, to avoid antagonizing or alienating specific sectors of society, and to enhance international legitimacy. Although Sandinista leaders trace much of their ideological inspiration to Augusto Sandino, the historical record shows that Sandino was not a Marxist-Leninist revolutionary. During his brief guerrilla war in the northern highlands from 1927–1934, Sandino's chief goal was Nicaraguan self-determination and the expulsion of U.S. influence.[13] The FSLN fostered political myths around Sandino in order to present their political program as a nationalist phenomenon and Sandino as the instigator of popular revolt culminating in the Sandinista revolution.[14]

Sandinismo became the application of Marxism-Leninism to Nicaraguan conditions, just as Maoism was the Chinese adaptation, and Castroism the Cuban variant. In the words of one FSLN statement,

> Sandino is above all a political, military, and ideological line, a model of action which has been followed and developed only by the national Sandinista Front, making it the sole trustee of the struggles, historical heritage, and revolutionary leadership of our people.[15]

In Marxism-Leninism the originators of *Sandinismo* had discovered a "comprehensive socioeconomic theory that explained the reasons for the poverty and political bankruptcy of Nicaragua while providing confident prediction of a better world to come."[16] The FSLN was deemed to be the instrumental factor in the country's development. All opposing political groups were "objectively" the representatives of imperialist and oligarchic interests. According to Sandinista historiography, the capitalist polarization of classes had not yet occurred in Nicaragua, as the bourgeoisie and proletariat remained weak forces: Hence, the "subjective factor" (the FSLN) was needed to intercede and hasten historical development not by stimulating the emergence of full-blown capitalism but by gradually establishing a socialist system while controlling and constraining the bourgeoisie. This represented Lenin's telescoping of the "bourgeois-democratic" stage of development. During a prolonged "transition phase," the "alliance of progressive forces" (the proletariat, peasantry, and patriotic bourgeoisie) would assist economic development while the Sandinistas expanded and consolidated their party-state. This period of transition "should not lead us to capitalism, reformism, nationalism, or any other development . . . our destination is socialism, a historically concrete mode of production and not a utopian society."[17]

Populism and nationalism have been closely interlinked by the Sandinistas with "anti-imperialism" and anti-Americanism. In their political pantheon, Sandino epitomized progressiveness and revolution while Somoza was the embodiment of stagnation and regression. Sandino's murder by the National Guard was blamed on the United States, while the Somoza dictatorship was purportedly created and controlled by Washington. In the words of the May 1977 FSLN General Political-Military Platform: "More than 40 years of *Somocista* dictatorial rule have allowed the subjugation of our nation by North American imperialism."[18] For the *Frente*, Nicaraguan "patriotism" was one local expression of revolutionary, socialist, or proletarian "internationalism" directed against "international capitalism." In Hollander's estimation the Sandinistas have tried to create "the image of a small, poor, victimized country, beset by economic difficulties caused by the guerrilla war (and the United States), of a government committed to political and economic pluralism, with leaders who were flexible egalitarian idealists inspired more by religion than Marxism-Leninism."[19] Conservative, liberal, and social democratic political parties seeking to establish a pluralistic system of government have been denounced as "anti-nationalist" and "pro-imperialist." Moreover, the radicalization and repressiveness of the regime have regularly been blamed on "foreign interference" and the "reactionary policies" of the domestic opposition against which the authorities have had to "protect the revolution."[20]

In a devoutly Catholic country, in which about 90 percent of the population actively profess their faith, the
FSLN has attempted to blend Christianity with *Sandinismo* to buttress support for the regime and weaken the position of the Catholic church hierarchy. Sandinista leaders
have avoided betraying their atheistic orientations and
masked their intention to undercut church authority over
the masses. "Sandinista Christians" have incorporated
many precepts of Latin America's "liberation theologians"
who implicitly support Marxist socialism in the Third
World. Fonseca considered it imperative to use "radical
Christianity" to neutralize the official church and to guarantee that no alternative religious-oriented reform movement
would emerge in the country.[21] A radical "people's church"
has been promoted to help extend the Sandinistas' base of
support and control. Religious elements have been included
in *Sandinismo* not to secularize the *Frente* but to make
Christianity synonymous with socialist revolution.[22] FSLN
propaganda fosters the impression that Marxism-Leninism
and Christianity are "revolutionary partners" on behalf of
the poor, in opposition to the church hierarchy, which supposedly protects the privileges of the rich. FSLN "liberation
theology" underscores that "love for the oppressed" has to
be expressed in revolutionary action aimed at a complete
overhaul of the political, economic, and social order. Instead
of banning religious rituals and symbols, the regime has
refurbished them with revolutionary content and reoriented
them toward the creation of a "new" or "socialist man." According to the "Sandinista Creed," the *Frente* represents the
vanguard of revolutionary Christianity leading the people
to the "true kingdom of God" – socialism on earth.[23]

Alliance Strategies of the FSLN

On the eve of their takeover the FSLN attempted to broad-
en its appeal by promising something to practically every
disgruntled social group, including land to the peasants,

higher wages for industrial workers, social services for the urban and rural poor, and free elections to the middle class. Capitalist entrepreneurs were also offered opportunities to participate in national reconstruction in order to attract them into FSLN-dominated alliances. In their dealings with non-Communists the comandantes saw little need to declare their doctrinal convictions and risk antagonism; it was much more advantageous to confuse potential opponents or co-opt them unwittingly to serve Sandinista interests.

Alliances with other political forces were intended to strengthen the appeal of *Sandinismo,* to gain recruits, and to neutralize opposition.[24] In October 1977 a front called "The Twelve" (*Los Doce*) was formed to incorporate prominent non-Sandinista figures who would speak out against Somoza in the international arena and garner support for the armed struggle. In March 1978 the United People's Movement (*Movimiento del Pueblo Unido* or MPU) combined 14 leftist political parties, labor unions, and student and youth groups to campaign for a "government of national unity" and draw support away from rival political forces. Having attracted non-Sandinistas into various coalitions, the Sandinistas aimed to erode these groups' political autonomy and capture their popular base. The alliance strategy with non-Communists led to the mistaken impression in some domestic and Western circles that the Sandinistas had evolved into a moderate "democratic socialist" or "nationalist" force. Nolan points out that the *terceristas* were wrongly identified by the Western media as favoring a non-capitalist and non-Communist "third way" development strategy and political structure.[25] The FSLN cultivated such an image and toned down its Marxist rhetoric, making sure that this change was understood internally as a tactical maneuver and not a political retreat.

After the takeover, the *Frente* maintained that power in Nicaragua was held by "the people" rather than any specific class; this encompassed all social forces "committed to the revolutionary process."[26] The links between them were supposedly "political-ideological" rather than "structural-economic," reflecting their support of the revolution. Conversely, all elements opposing the revolution, irrespective of their class position, could be placed "objectively" outside "the camp of the people." All social sectors were therefore judged by their malleability and utility to the comandantes.

2

Sandinismo: The Levers of Control

The Sandinistas' agrarian and ethnic policies cannot be evaluated without surveying the mechanisms of political and social control the FSLN has imposed on Nicaraguan society as a whole during the past decade. The Sandinistas' professed long-term objective is the construction of a Leninist party-state and a loosely defined "socialist mode of production." In the words of Orlando Nunez and Roger Burbach, the "political revolution" was merely the seizure of power by a revolutionary vanguard; "the 'social revolution' is the subsequent transformation of society and the effort to build a socialist order."[1] The FSLN realized the limitations on rapid communization arising from Nicaragua's economic underdevelopment and geopolitical placement, as well as the initial weakness of the government in conducting such a task; it thus decided to maintain its "class alliances" while focusing on extending its political controls over both state and society.

The *Frente* denied that Nicaragua had to pass through advanced capitalist development before embarking on socialism. In its estimation the countries of Latin America were already incorporated as exploited dependencies in the world capitalist system, though internally they exhibited many features of precapitalism. The FSLN had a historic

obligation to hasten the political, social, and economic met-
amorphosis that the indigenous bourgeoisie was unable to
accomplish under Somoza and that the proletariat was too
weak to undertake.[2] According to Comandante Bayardo
Arce the three principles espoused by the FSLN during its
drive for power (nonalignment abroad, political pluralism,
and a mixed economy) were tactical devices to disarm internal opposition and make the Sandinistas respectable inter-
nationally while Leninization would proceed under the
covers.[3]

The *Frente's* "national unity" project resulted in provisional "class co-existence without class conciliation, expressing the hegemony of the popular camp and the political sub-
ordination of the bourgeoisie."[4] Reneging on promises of a
representative democracy, the FSLN inaugurated a "popular-
democratic phase" in which political opposition was to be
gradually disarmed, Sandinista control extended, and the
foundations of a planned economy laid. Limited pluralism
and tolerance for a private economic sector were "necessary
in the current stage of the revolution, a stage that will be
surpassed when certain economic conditions are achieved in
the country."[5]

Political Control

To neutralize alternative parties, the Sandinistas adopted
customary Leninist "magnet tactics" to co-opt useful collaborators and "salami tactics" to stifle their former allies. During the late 1970s, various "radical Christians" were incorporated into the movement to broaden its appeal; they also
proved valuable in attacking the official church. Social dem-
ocrats and liberals were also enticed into the Sandinista
orbit to gain credibility for the FSLN and to detach them
from the enfeebled opposition parties. The *Frente* itself
"was gradually redesigned as an organization of concentric
circles: an outer ring of sympathizers and collaborators, an

intermediate structure of ideological militants, and a directive nucleus of committed Marxist-Leninists."[6] Such an arrangement supported the impression that the Sandinistas were not a sectarian Marxist force but a movement of radical social reformers.

Several non-Sandinistas originally held posts in various government bodies but were later pushed out or left voluntarily because of mounting disagreements with the comandantes.[7] Those who openly opposed the regime's political orientation were displaced, but this pruning process was usually as gradual as possible "in order to avoid uniting in a single front all the adversaries, present and future, of the revolution."[8] Democratic parties were distanced from the policy-making process, and much of their organizational structure was paralyzed. Several of these parties later forged the oppositionist umbrella group, the Nicaraguan Democratic Coordinator (*Coordinadora Democrática Nicaragüense* or CDN). The Sandinistas have also made use of a leftist opposition that is generally supportive of their policies and in some cases advocates more radical measures.[9] With declared opponents on the left, the FSLN is able to reinforce publicly its aura of centrism and moderation.

By mid-1980, seven of the comandantes had assumed key government positions, and the ruling Governing Junta of National Reconstruction (*Junta de Gobierno de Reconstrucción Nacional* or JGRN) was under firm FSLN control. Although tolerating small and largely ineffectual parties in the semi-legislative National Assembly, the *Frente* gained full charge over all executive and legislative branches of government. Token pluralism was preserved to avert alienating the relatively small professional and administrative class necessary for postwar reconstruction. All tolerated parties were required to espouse programs corresponding to the FSLN platform or at least not contradicting government policy. Sandinista objectives were disguised behind a democratic veneer needed during periods of instability and external threat:

> A successful consolidation and stabilization of power requires that Marxist-Leninists conceal their true intentions and convey the impression that a current, temporary, transitional phase masked by a residual pluralism and capitalism is a new, permanent hybrid of socialism and capitalism.[10]

Behind the cover of a "state of emergency," first imposed in early 1982 and regularly extended ever since, police powers have been extended and numerous civil rights restricted or suspended – including freedom of movement, assembly, association, and communication.[11] In practice, these emergency measures simply formalized already existing limitations on political freedoms. The mechanisms of FSLN control were in fact implanted prior to any hostile U.S. involvement or the emergence of the contras as a viable fighting force.

By employing selective rather than mass repression, the Sandinistas have often confounded critics, confused international public opinion, and created fear and uncertainty in society. Joshua Muravchik points out that the FSLN conducts a "reign of intimidation" rather than a "reign of terror." Terror itself is employed selectively and usually in areas outside the international spotlight.[12] Compared with many other newly established Communist states, Nicaragua has displayed some refinement in its dealings with critics, relying on intimidation rather than swift liquidation. Managua's political prisoners, for example, whose total has varied from a few dozen to several thousand, are usually low- or middle-ranking opposition activists outside the media limelight. In addition, countless numbers of suspected citizens have been arbitrarily detained for "counter-revolutionary" activities, interrogated, threatened, and released, but few have been killed. The better known dissidents are mostly persecuted through administrative and economic sanctions rather than outright coercion.

Aside from such repression, the Interior Ministry has sponsored *turbas divinas* or mobs of youths that harass and assault preselected targets. The *turbas* supposedly display the strength of spontaneous "people's power" against "reactionaries" while disguising the government's role in browbeating its opponents.

With regard to the church, the FSLN has refrained from overt and sweeping persecution, which would have immediately estranged large sectors of the population from the regime. Instead, it has sought to subvert the authority and cohesiveness of the institution through infiltration, propaganda, disruption, and selective attacks on particularly troublesome clergymen. Furthermore, the government-sponsored People's Church (*Iglesia Popular*) has been pitted against the Catholic hierarchy, including the widely respected Cardinal Miguel Obando y Bravo. Its influence has been promoted through the mass media, government-controlled "theological centers," and networks of neighborhood "religious groups" espousing "liberation theology." The "people's church" champions all Sandinista policies and has been provided with large funds to reinterpret the gospel according to revolutionary guidelines. Its sway among Catholics has proved unimpressive, however, and the official church continues to command the loyalty of the bulk of Nicaraguan society.

The Sandinistas have proceeded steadily and prudently in constructing a Leninist-type mass party during their gradual socialist transformation. The vanguard nucleus has perceived no urgent need for a large and potentially cumbersome political organization, given the shortage of well-prepared recruits. The premature creation and declaration of a Sandinista Party would also have left Managua prone to charges of constructing a totalitarian state and may have quickly alienated non-Communist collaborators and foreign supporters. Internal Leninization has therefore proceeded in stages with the careful selection, indoctrination, and training of suitable cadres.

Among the organizational changes in the *Frente* geared toward party building, one can note the creation of a national secretariat and of three commissions for political affairs, defense and security, and state affairs assigned to the FSLN's ruling body, the DN. The Political Commission became the DN's executive organ or a self-appointed inner cabinet overseeing the other commissions. It was later replaced by an Executive Committee consisting of the DN's five top comandantes entrusted with "organizing the execution and control of decisions in all instances of revolutionary power." Below this level various departments dealing with such matters as propaganda, recruitment, and political education were created.

As in other Leninist parties "democratic centralism" was instituted within the FSLN, involving hierarchical decision making and strict internal discipline. The appointment of officials to all regional, zonal, and "base" FSLN committees is decided directly by the next highest level; a similar procedure is evident within the government-sponsored mass organizations. Every FSLN member belongs to a "base committee" formed in his or her neighborhood, work place, or military unit and directed by an assigned political secretary. Ideological commitment and obedience are deemed paramount for any high position in the *Frente*:

> It is right that we demand in our ranks more (regarding) standards and party life, more class consciousness and more Marxist ideological clarity, but let us not do this on an open and mass level, since we run the danger of becoming sectarian and isolating ourselves from the masses.[13]

Before it seized power, the FSLN had only about 500 fully fledged cadres. By 1984 the *Frente* numbered approximately 10,000 core militants, about 50,000 general members, and several thousand active supporters.[14] Three distinct stages of Sandinista commitment are prescribed: aspirant, FSLN member, and militant. Militants have undergone intensive training in party schools, and their devotion has been tested "in the field." Militants must exhibit unquestionable loyalty and a track record of activism before assuming any full-time office in the political apparatus. Although cadre training takes place at all organizational levels, a thorough verification process precedes membership in the inner Sandinista sanctum. As in other Leninist pyramids, occasional purges are also conducted to root out unreliable and undisciplined functionaries.

The periodic FSLN Assemblies of Cadres and Militants are staging posts en route to a more coherent future party organization. The Sandinista Assembly, consisting of about 100 *Frente* notables such as military officers, departmental officials, and heads of mass organizations, resembles an embryonic Central Committee. As a "consultative body" it provides recommendations to the DN but has little ultimate control over the comandantes' decisions. The FSLN is ostensibly developing "to the maximum its organic structure until it becomes an iron-hard Leninist Party" steeped with "Marxist-Leninist norms of party life."[15] The process is likely to be prolonged and arduous, however, given the rudimentary state of "revolutionary consciousness" among wide sectors of society.

Legislative Control

Since 1979 the governmental structure has been subordinated to the FSLN through direct organizational control and the placement of Sandinista cadres in all important posts from which they supervise state functions. The quasi-legislative Council of State was dominated by *Frente* members and supporters and primarily verified amendments to laws promulgated by the DN. The council was replaced in December 1984 by the National Assembly, a nominal parliamentary body regulated by the FSLN.

Election procedures have been closely controlled by the Sandinistas, including the November 1984 presidential ballot after which the governing JGRN was superseded by a new cabinet steered by President and Comandante Daniel Ortega. The elections restricted participation by the splintered opposition after the most substantial rival parties had been disqualified. The discreet use of coercion, manipulation, and censorship helped ensure that the FSLN would not be formally voted out of power.[16] A similar process may be expected during the run-up to the February 1990 presidential elections.

During the past decade the regime has proceeded to enmesh state institutions and social activities in its web of control. It has benefited from the experience of Soviet bloc advisers attached to various government organs. FSLN leaders have obstructed any legislation to formalize or define the separation of party and state. For instance, the August 1983 law on political parties made no distinction between the Sandinista revolution, the FSLN itself, and the Nicaraguan state. The state administration tripled in size during the first year, in many cases employing former Somoza bureaucrats. An elite Communist-type *nomenklatura* is being formed in most arenas of public life with its associated powers, privileges, and patronage networks. The regime created nine regional governments to enhance the expanding state structure and to "consolidate the state apparatus politically and administratively at the municipal level."[17]

The Sandinista judicial structure has increasingly "departed from a civil law system (and) assumed the role of an instrument for the consolidation of the FSLN's political power."[18] Some observers conclude that "Sandinista law" has been more arbitrary than Somoza's procedures and has imposed its political will more systematically than did Somoza. Managua has sought to instill the notion that the FSLN is the one true source of law from which all citizens' rights emanate. Although the Supreme Court retained some autonomy from the regime, its powers have been gradually curtailed and superseded by an alternative, politicized judicial process. The official "people's courts" are presided over by politically loyal judges employing the vaguely worded Public Order Law to prosecute Sandinista opponents. In addition, the Anti-Somocista Tribunals were purportedly established to punish former National Guardsmen, but they became a means for dealing with any political rivals and systematically violated the principles of elementary justice.

FSLN control has also been augmented through various mass organizations and supervisory organs. The Sandinista Defense Committees (*Comités de Defensa Sandinista* or CDS) have been formed in all urban neighborhoods and many rural areas as part of the regime's security and surveillance apparatus; they are modeled on the Cuban block committees. In addition to civil defense functions, the CDS conducts intelligence gathering and counterintelligence work, dispenses ration cards and licenses, and supervises food distribution, price controls, and job placements. About 15,000 CDS operated as the "eyes and ears" of the FSLN with a total membership of some 600,000 people by the mid-1980s. A host of other mass organizations, embracing rural and urban workers, women, youth, children, and professionals, act as "transmission belts" for explaining and implementing *Frente* policy. This form of "popular democracy" dispenses with a genuinely representative pluralistic system and facilitates direct political control over the masses. All mass associations are overseen by a DN subcommittee, while the Sandinista Assembly determines all appointments, issues policy guidelines, and closely supervises their work. The basic principles of the mass organizations are democratic centralism, collective leadership, and a politically determined system of appointments at local, municipal, departmental, and national levels.[19] They contribute to the "mass struggle" without enlarging the FSLN or diluting its internal discipline and are considered training grounds for Sandinista membership.

Sandinization has also been advanced by the DN's direct control over all security mechanisms including the military, militia, and police forces. The Sandinista Popular Army (*Ejercito Popular Sandinista* or EPS) was established in September 1979 around a core of FSLN guerrilla leaders. By 1986 it numbered nearly 75,000 active duty soldiers and more than 200,000 reservists; by comparison the National Guard at its peak did not exceed 10,000 members.[20] According to article 177 of the FSLN's draft constitution, the Sandinista army is a "strategic instrument of national defense and revolutionary gains."[21] The Sandinista Popular Militia (*Milicia Popular Sandinista* or MPS) was created in February 1980 when the FSLN faced no major armed threat. It numbers about 100,000 regulars and reservists and provides auxiliaries for the army and police. The MPS is particularly active in rural areas protecting government buildings and cooperatives, engaging in anti-contra drives, and suppressing local opposition. Political sections exist in all military, militia, and police units to help politicize young conscripts.

Economic Control

Economic levers have also been employed to further FSLN control, stifle organized opposition, and maintain productivity during the gradual transition to socialism. Nicaragua's economic transformation is defined as a variant of "noncapitalist development" that exploits a restricted capitalist sector devoid of political power. In the aftermath of the takeover, no extensive nationalization program or rapid socialization of the means of production was undertaken so as not to alienate capital and labor or frighten off foreign investment and assistance. Instead, the temporary alliance with private capital was intended to "buy the Revolution time and breathing space, in which the class character of the process can consolidate itself and the class struggle be played out on favorable terms."[22] The state is steadily to become the "center of capital accumulation," gradually reducing the role of capitalists during the introduction of a centrally steered economy: "the state and cooperative properties will be hegemonic, coexisting with medium and small and even large private production, in which the backward relations of capitalism will surely become secondary, subordinated."[23]

Sandinista socialization has proceeded more hesitantly in the economic realm than in the political sphere, once the regime nationalized the financial system, foreign trade, and the mining, fisheries, and forestry industries. Detailed economic planning has remained rudimentary, with the economic role of the state mostly limited to implementing fiscal and monetary policies and managing state properties. In contrast to the situation in Cuba, in which capitalism virtually disappeared within two years of Castro's victory, FSLN plans called for the reduced private sector to be controlled indirectly and used to the advantage of the state. The bourgeoisie could maintain its means of production and continue drawing profits, but was deprived of political clout or decision-making powers over the national economy. Weber depicts this as a slow transition to socialism that gradually alters the "balance of forces" rather than a head-on confrontation with nonstate sectors.[24] Managua's "mixed economy" strategy has misled some commentators into concluding that a novel and exemplary economic model had been devised. Conversely, it has been attacked by more orthodox Communists for its internal contradictions and timidity in launching the transition to socialism.[25]

The loosely defined "mixed economy" consists of three main sectors. First, there is state ownership of the "commanding heights," including major national industries and about 25 percent of cultivated land for agro-exporting. Second, the regime has encouraged cooperative ventures as a preliminary form of collectivization in the countryside. Third, the FSLN tolerates private businesses whose profits can be siphoned off through taxation and that can foster economic growth or at least prevent economic decline. The capitalist sector provides a vital source of contact with foreign investors and aid donors; its preservation deflects international criticism of Sandinista policies. Forrest Colburn estimates that small states like Nicaragua lack the necessary resources to pursue a fully independent development strategy based on full state control in the early stages of political consolidation.[26] According to the FSLN's political-military platform, "Nicaraguan capitalism, unlike that of Europe and other highly developed and industrialized nations, does not facilitate the immediate establishment of socialism."[27] Although the bourgeoisie will evidently not be allowed to "reproduce as a class," its demise does not seem to be tied to a predetermined time scale; much depends on its continuing usefulness to the regime and on prevailing domestic and geopolitical conditions.

Even though Managua requires foreign capitalist assistance and domestic entrepreneurial, technical, and managerial skills to rebuild the economy before proceeding to a "higher state of development," the Sandinistas clearly fear an expanding and politically vibrant private sector. In the long term, according to the regime, individual and collective property "must fulfill a social function by virtue of which it can be subject to limitations on its title, enjoyment, use, and alienability whether for reasons of security, public interest, or utility, social interest . . . or for the purpose of agrarian reform."[28]

The extent and durability of private property has remained vague in official statements, as all forms of ownership must supposedly "benefit the people" at the regime's discretion. Article 99 of the 1987 constitution underscores that state direction and planning of the national economy are intended to "guarantee and defend the interests of the majority."[29] Since the early 1980s, various administrative, legal, and fiscal constraints have been placed on the independent economic sector. With the lack of long-term security of capital, the general economic disorder, the uncertainty about future state policies, and the decline in financial incentives, the Sandinista system has proved unattractive to much of the bourgeoisie. Many urban and rural entrepreneurs have fled abroad, restricted their production, or had their property confiscated by the state.

3

Sandinista Policies: The Peasantry

Agriculture is the key sector in Nicaragua's economy. Today, as in 1979, about 60 to 70 percent of Nicaragua's nearly 3 million people obtain the bulk of their resources directly from the land.[1] Roughly half of them are peasants or *campesinos* – direct agrarian producers cultivating parcels of land that they own or rent.

On the eve of the Sandinista takeover, the remaining 30 to 40 percent of Nicaragua's rural population included large and medium-sized "capitalist" landowners, seasonal farm workers, and full-time plantation wage laborers. A large proportion of the peasant proprietors also engaged in temporary or seasonal forms of wage labor to supplement their subsistence incomes.

Before 1979, Nicaragua's agricultural economy was dominated neither by foreign corporations nor by large quasi-feudal *haciendas*. During the previous 30 years the latter had been gradually displaced by capitalist agro-export farming on *latifundios*, or large estates. By 1978, the "rural bourgeoisie" accounted for about 9 percent of the rural population; it owned 84.8 percent of the nation's farmland and focused on agro-exporting. The bourgeoisie included large owners with holdings in excess of 350 acres and small and medium-sized owners with farms ranging in size from 17 to 340 acres.[2] Much of the traditional subsistence cultivation by peasants was therefore superseded by the growth of large cotton and coffee plantations, with agro-exports accounting for about 70 percent of Nicaragua's foreign exchange earnings. The paternalistic agrarian class system was largely replaced by market-based capitalist relations.

With increasing urbanization, modernization, and economic development between 1960 and 1970 the landowning peasant population declined from about 60 percent to 40 percent of the national total. The large stratum of rural dwellers therefore included *minifundistas* with tiny plots (numbering about half of the rural populace and occupying more than 15 percent of the cultivable land) and a class of permanent or temporary wage laborers (amounting to 32 percent of all rural residents).[3] Throughout the 1970s the agrarian population experienced a steady fall in living standards as the production of basic foodstuffs failed to keep pace with population growth.

With the development of sizable agro-export concerns since the 1940s, thousands of small farms were swallowed up. The dispossessed peasants either joined the ranks of the rural proletariat and petty artisans in the urban *barrios* (neighborhoods) or migrated to the "agricultural frontier" in the highland, northern, and eastern parts of the country. The central highland region and its peripheries generally remained subsistence-oriented with little economic infrastructure, capital investment, urbanization, or technological development. By contrast, the Pacific coastal zones contained a preponderant "semi-proletariat" reliant on seasonal work on coffee and cotton plantations. A large stratum of the agrarian populace in the central areas consisted of "middle peasants" dependent on cattle rearing and coffee production primarily for exports.

In overall national terms, by the late 1970s the owners of large and medium farms engaged in export-focused agriculture; poor peasants with small holdings relied on more traditional staples for basic subsistence or on local markets; landless seasonal laborers were employed in the large agro-exporting units. Peasant proprietors themselves could be usefully subdivided into "rich peasants" who permanently or seasonally hired varying numbers of farmhands, "middle-level" or largely self-sufficient households, and smallholders who engaged in periodic wage labor for other agrarian strata.

Before 1979, practically the only regions with an authentic full-time "rural proletariat" were the cotton fields of Leon and Chinandega departments. The majority of farm laborers were only partially proletarianized and maintained various additional productive activities. Only about 20 percent of the nation's population could be described as proletarian in the strict Marxist sense. Nicaragua had not significantly developed such basic industries as metallurgy or machine building; industrialization was mostly limited to small manufacturers, food processing, and packaging. Even though nearly half of the population lived in cities by the mid-1970s, the majority of this economically active population (EAP) pursued small-scale artisanship and trading or was self-employed in various service ventures.

Rural Control

In tracing the evolution of the Sandinistas' agrarian programs, it is important to remember that in their theoretical writings and policy statements FSLN leaders have propounded an eventual "radical transformation" of the entire rural sector. In the *Frente's* "worker-peasant alliance," the proletariat evidently constitutes the "fundamental force" of the revolution, while other "popular sectors," including the peasantry and urban petty-bourgeoisie, represent the "principle force" because of their numerical size and usefulness for the Sandinistas. FSLN comandantes, including Agriculture Minister Jaime Wheelock, have embellished their essentially Marxist-Leninist standpoints regarding the peasantry during the "transitional period" of necessary class alliances.[4] Throughout this phase, the "mixed economy" model was to assist the state in its steadfast socialization program but without necessitating wholesale and "premature" mass collectivization in the countryside. The Sandinistas thereby hoped to avoid the extensive social disruption and enormous material losses sustained by the Soviet Union, the People's Republic of China, and various Third World Leninist regimes in the early stages of their political consolidation. According to E. V. K. Fitzgerald, the process of nationalization and socialization was not to proceed faster than the capacity of the state to assimilate the private sector while avoiding a massive collapse in agricultural exports and domestic food supplies.[5]

During the indefinite "transitional phase," the assurance of overall government control over the rural population has been a principal concern for Managua. This control has been furthered since 1979 through the FSLN's local government juntas, the CDS, the mass organizations, and numerous repressive techniques discussed in the previous chapter. Mass mobilization measures have been employed to raise "revolutionary consciousness," help recruit "voluntary labor" for "patriotic duties," and extend Communist indoctrination throughout the countryside. Soon after the takeover, the Rural Workers' Association (*Associación de Trabajadores del Campo* or ATC) became a chief political instrument for the regime, especially among the rural proletariat, seasonal farm workers, and small farmers. Established in March 1978 by FSLN militants and radical Christian groups as a "class based organization," the ATC reached 58,000 members in 1979, 106,000 in 1981, and 135,000 in 1986. Its current size reportedly exceeds 150,000, though it has forfeited some of its members to another official mass organization established for landowning farmers.

According to *Frente*, "our organizational efforts among the proletariat, both urban and rural, should be the central axis of all our work among the masses."[6] The regime's long-term objective appears to be an amalgamation of the major labor unions into one centralized national federation along traditional Leninist lines. Such plans remain impractical in the immediate future, however, given the country's diverse occupational and productive structure.

In the first few years of Sandinista rule, the ATC was used to promote the "class struggle" in rural areas by championing land confiscations, ousting anti-FSLN activists, campaigning against "bourgeois values," and dissipating peasant resistance to agrarian cooperativization. In addition to organizing the agrarian labor force in Sandinista-sponsored activities, helping to enforce the prohibition on strikes and other protests, and participating in the management of state farms and cooperatives, the ATC was empowered to report on peasant and capitalist "misdemeanors" that could make the culprits liable to expropriation and other official sanctions. For ATC officials Nicaragua's agrarian reforms were not merely an economic endeavor to promote rural development, but indispensable measures for completing the "cultural, intellectual, technical, social, and political transformation of the peasants."[7] FSLN mass organizations are generally geared toward extending support for and increasing dependence on the state. The ATC itself encountered little organized opposition or competition, as no independent rural unions functioned under Somoza and their emergence was largely thwarted by the new regime. The official body found it easier, however, to recruit and mobilize the more geographically concentrated rural laborers than the more dispersed small and medium-sized peasant farmers.

Militarization and Mass Mobilization

Militarization became a key FSLN tool for mass mobilization, regimentation, and social control in the countryside. The size of the armed forces increased more than twelvefold between 1979 and 1985, when it peaked at around 75,000 active duty personnel. Since the early days of *Sandinismo*, militarism has constituted a central organizational ingredient. Commitment to the armed struggle has been perceived as an almost purifying experience for the FSLN because the discipline of the armed forces evidently facilitates class consciousness, political indoctrination, cadre training, and "democratic centralism" in the absence of a mass Leninist-type party. The Nicaraguan opposition has consistently objected to Managua's version of military conscription as a violation of freedom of association that forces youths into a politically partisan army. In George Black's estimation, "military training intermingles with constant political education"; each recruit is subjected to regular spells of ideological instruction by political commissars attached to each military unit.[8] The military draft law of 1983 lowered the age of conscription to 17 and involved 2 years of "patriotic military service" for any young man between 17 and 25.

Tens of thousands of Nicaraguans have passed through the armed forces and thereby experienced intensive political indoctrination. In the absence of a sizable revolutionary proletariat,

> The army, and not the factory, is the primary school of socialist politics. Not only is the lived experience of the early vanguard leadership that of an urban or rural guerrilla force, but the second generation of leaders, the whole third force, and the masses of youth have as their principal tutor the war effort against imperialist aggression. The code for socialist participation, learned through the organizational structure of the army, will be the model for the future society because the heroes of the war are destined to occupy the leadership posts after the peace is won.[9]

Although there is a distinct romanticism among some Western Marxists regarding the nobility and achievements of Sandinista militarism, Peter Marchetti's summation gives a useful indicator of some of the political rather than military objectives of FSLN army training.

The military mobilization of thousands of young adult males has also had an adverse impact on agricultural production. According to Fitzgerald, it has reduced the size of the available labor force, disrupted output, uprooted peasants, and made it difficult to reintegrate soldiers back into civilian life, particularly in agriculture.[10] In the Sandinista view, the political, ideological, and security benefits deriving from extensive militarization evidently offset the costs of economic dislocation.

Rural Education Campaigns

An important FSLN political device designed to enmesh the rural population in the emerging party-state has revolved around literacy campaigns, educational programs, and social welfare schemes. The mid-1980s mass literacy campaign among *campesinos* was a loudly orchestrated public relations exercise intended to garner popular support for the regime through official displays of concern for the rural poor.[11] Managua enlisted Catholic church support and international funding for the crusade, from which the FSLN gained most of the positive publicity. The campaign was also a means for mobilizing thousands of university and high school students in the FSLN's "political project." It became a useful method for strengthening the political commitment of urban youths in the Popular Literacy Army (*Ejercito Popular de Alfabetización* or EPA) closely monitored by Sandinista militants. The EPA has also served as a valuable recruiting ground for the official youth organization, the July 19th Sandinista Youth (*Juventud Sandinista 19 de Julio* or JS-19).

Although the government claimed that illiteracy had been lowered from 55 percent to about 13 percent during the course of the campaign, it is difficult to verify such contentions objectively or to assess the degree of literacy attained. Indeed "literacy" has often amounted to little more than the ability to recite simple Sandinista slogans learned in crash indoctrination courses. The educational fragility of the crusade has even been officially admitted on occasion. Mass organizations have been energized to assist in "follow-up programs" and in the creation of "learning groups" and adult education classes in the Popular Education Collectives (*Colectivo de Educación Popular* or CEP). Indoctrination through "noncapitalist education" has been pursued among all sectors of society to help root out "neocolonial penetration of Nicaraguan culture." The Ministry of Education has made it mandatory for all college students to study "scientific Marxism-Leninism," while all educational material published with Cuban aid extols the FSLN as the sole "people's vanguard."

The Nicaraguan educational system has apparently become "one of the key settings of the ideological class struggle." It enables Managua to spread its political controls to even the remotest rural areas and helps create a network of *Frente* watchdogs and informers behind the facade of a progressive humanitarian crusade.[12] Other social welfare campaigns designed to implant positive attitudes toward the regime and consolidate government control in the countryside, while reportedly improving health care and reducing disease, have included rural health clinics, vaccination drives, neighborhood clean-up operations, and hygiene workshops. These programs dispense medicines with heavy doses of political propaganda, provide activists with a sense of purpose and achievement, and bolster the Sandinista local organizations and their social control networks.

Agrarian Reforms

In the view of the FSLN, only the proletariat "will go all the way" toward socialism once it is fully "class conscious," politicized, and organized by the Communists.[13] The remaining social classes, including the *campesinos*, have to be inculcated with the avowed discipline and self-denial of the idealized "socialist worker." To accomplish this mammoth undertaking in economically unfavorable circumstances requires that the "socialization of agriculture" proceed in stages. Indeed, the authorities have displayed a great deal of flexibility in their agrarian reforms and their promotion of a socialized work force. In seeking to avoid major disruptions in output, they have taken account of domestic conditions and international perceptions and realized that outright coercion could prove counterproductive.

In February 1985, Comandante Victor Tirado announced that during the "prolonged transition stage" a private farming sector would have to be tolerated because the government could not currently organize all economic activities.[14] According to FSLN spokesmen, the "mixed economy" model will only be superseded "once the country reaches other economic conditions." The precise nature of such conditions has not been specified, nor has the date of their expected crystallization. In the short term, the Sandinistas would make provisional concessions and implement land reforms to entice private farmers into a closer dependence on the government. Such compromises would be progressively eroded and discarded until the state and cooperative sectors could squeeze out private production altogether and fully control all agricultural surpluses. This process could be long, however, and could be subject to reverses because of the need to maintain sufficient production levels.

Various provisions of the agrarian reform program were designed to keep socialist construction on track even when the "locomotive of history" was slowed down. The March 1980 law on "decapitalization and economic sabotage" stipulated the imposition of fines, imprisonment, and state expropriation against anyone in the private sector who did not comply with official regulations regarding production, trading, and investment policies. Public criticisms of the regime could also provide sufficient grounds for the confiscation of farms. Such rulings left the door open to arbitrary land seizures and socialization. In fact, between 1979 and 1984, more than one-third of all farmland was reportedly confiscated by the state.

The nationalization of the financial system resulted in the creation of a state holding company, the Nicaraguan

Finance Corporation (CORFIN), which allocates credit "in accordance with the goals of the Sandinista development model."[15] The financing of agriculture has been dominated by the National Development Bank, which has consistently favored "cooperative forms of production" in the allocation of credits and has discriminated against large private farming on political grounds. The pace of land confiscation owing to purportedly inefficient use increased significantly in the mid-1980s. A January 1986 legal amendment to the agrarian reforms allowed for the appropriation of "mismanaged, idle or underdeveloped land" or land "needed for public use." Even productively exploited acreage could be bought or confiscated by the state under special conditions – for example, for the resettlement of war refugees or for distribution to landless peasants in areas of high population density. Simultaneously, rights of land inheritance have been restricted and land taxes raised for many capitalist owners.

The expropriation of large *latifundios*, particularly those owned by Somoza, his family, close associates, and members of the National Guard, took place between 1979 and 1981. These profitable export-oriented agricultural concerns, which accounted for about 20 percent of gross agricultural output and less than 20 percent of cultivable land, were transferred to the People's Property Area (*Area de Propiedad del Pueblo* or APP) state farms and not distributed to small peasant producers. The regime expected the new units to become the center of agricultural growth, capital formation, and modernization, while resolving the problem of rural unemployment and facilitating agrarian proletarianization. The growth in state farm employment leveled off soon after the dispossession of Somoza's holdings, however, in the light of the APP's unimpressive economic results. Managua instead focused on milking profits from the more productive independent farming sector while promoting a gradual increase in cooperative farming.

The initial transfer of large estates to direct state management was only partly a question of supposed economic rationality, especially as some parceling and redistribution of these modernized capital-intensive units may have actually enhanced agricultural output. In many cases, *campesinos* who had occupied *Somocista* lands during the insurrection were required to give them up to the state. This created confusion, resentment, friction, and some overt opposition among the peasantry about the Sandinistas' sudden resistance to land redistribution.

> Not only did [the FSLN] prefer collective production in cooperatives or on state farms for ideological reasons, [it] also feared that granting land to individual peasants would lead to the "repeasantization" of what [it] thought was a substantially proletarianized rural work force and reduce the availability of labor for the export sector.[16]

The government wished to avoid stimulating the growth of small and medium-sized peasant holdings. It was not in its interest to encourage either capitalist expansion in the countryside or increasing class polarization between an independent peasantry and state supervised wage workers. Such uncontrolled developments may have accentuated political instability and opposition to the recently installed regime. In Black's estimation, *Frente* leaders considered that "there was no deeply rooted property instinct among Nicaraguan peasants, and that agrarian reform might therefore move directly from *latifundismo* to collectivization, without passing first through a phase of redistribution of land into privately owned parcels."[17]

This initially doctrinaire stance was modified by the Sandinistas in the early 1980s so as not to alienate dramatically the land-hungry peasants and cause a dramatic fall in food output and export earnings during the precarious "transitional phase." FSLN policymakers now argued that because capitalism raises the productivity of agrarian labor it was carrying out "historically progressive" tasks that should be closely monitored but not halted by the revolu-

tion.[18] The glaring contradiction between official concessions to private farming and the goal of socialized agriculture has never been satisfactorily resolved by the regime.
Instead it has led to simmering conflicts with both the
large agro-exporting businessmen and the smaller landowning peasantry.

The most technically efficient and profitable sectors of
private farming that harvest major crops for substantial
export earnings or for domestic consumption have been tolerated by the FSLN. In some instances they were offered
credit and pricing incentives to raise output, and no ceilings
were imposed on productive holdings. The regime opposed
land seizures by poor peasants from "patriotic" large landowners in order not to antagonize its anti-Somoza "rural
bourgeois allies," to maintain agro-exporting, and to prevent
the burgeoning of the small peasantry. Nevertheless, the
Ministry of Foreign Trade (*Ministerio de Comercio Exterior*
or MICE) acquired a monopoly over exporting, while indi-
rect state control over the private sector was ensured
through taxation, price setting, input allocation, and the
determination of the volume of crops purchased from large
farmers. Instead of facing outright expropriation, the
agrarian capitalists were primarily required to administer
their units of production and enter into "production agreements" with the authorities. They were guaranteed a modest profit by state officials, but had to relinquish any political or economic ambitions.

The limited and conditional forms of government support have failed to reassure landowners, especially with the
ever-present threat of confiscation if productivity declines
or if the political climate deteriorates. Between 1979 and
1985, large private farms of more than 340 acres declined
from about 52 percent of cultivable land to 24 percent. During the same period, small and medium-sized peasant farms
of 17 to 340 acres declined from 46 to 43 percent. The
private sector has endeavored to maintain a sufficient yield
to avoid expropriation in the absence of any long-term profit incentives to intensify cultivation and output. The

wealthier farmers have cut back their investments by reducing the size of their herds and the acreage planted and by selling off farm machinery. They remain understandably unwilling to take financial risks in an unstable political and economic climate in which renewed state intervention cannot be discounted. This has led to an overall decline in agricultural yields.[19] Many landowners have remained in the country only because they fear confiscation from not cultivating their farms; meanwhile they hope for an eventual change of government.[20]

Although the majority of middle and small peasants have not faced outright state expropriation or "dekulakization," they have encountered numerous economic pressures and constraints intended to discourage expansion. These include set harvest delivery quotas to state agencies, high taxation, and low prices for farm produce. Such levers enable the government to extract a significant portion of the peasants' surplus and control many aspects of their labor process without necessitating direct state involvement in production. The Nicaraguan Basic Foodstuffs Company (*Empresa Nicaragüense de Alimentos Básicos* or ENABAS), under the control of the Ministry of Internal Trade (*Ministerio de Comercio Interior* or MICOIN), was formed in 1980 to purchase a large portion of the food harvest from the peasantry and thereby also help restrict the role of private middlemen and market vendors. This strategy expedited the imposition of centralized price controls and obstructed traditional market mechanisms in the countryside.

Yet the official collection and distribution of agricultural produce has been beset by incompetence and mismanagement. ENABAS initially attempted to centralize grain procurement without developing a large and dependable transportation network and storage facilities to handle the load. Substantial waste resulted, as well as a disruption of essential supplies. Eventually the authorities created a network of intermediate collection centers dispersed throughout the country to purchase grain and sell consumer goods to the peasants. Although not severe enough to eliminate private farming altogether, low purchase prices have acted as disincentives for smallholders to increase output much beyond their immediate needs.

The disbursement of credits by government banks to the independent peasantry has also been manipulated to encourage farmers to affiliate with the Sandinista mass organizations. In many instances refusal to cooperate with the ATC or other official bodies has resulted in a loss of credits and other economic penalties. Moreover, the granting of reasonably liberal credits in the first two years of FSLN rule contributed little to stimulating production, as farmers of all sizes had few long-term material incentives to raise productivity. Many of them registered their resistance to official policy by withholding produce from the state, decreasing the size of cultivated land, or gradually withdrawing from farming altogether. Managua's various agrarian reforms thereby actually curtailed the output of foodstuffs for domestic consumption.

Unionization

The National Union of Farmers and Ranchers (*Union Nacional de Agricultores y Ganaderos* or UNAG) was established in April 1981 to ensure state supervision over small and medium producers who could not be easily accommodated in the ATC. UNAG enrolled about 42,000 farmers by 1982, 75,000 by 1983, and more than 120,000 by 1985, constituting about one quarter of the economically active rural population.[21] One of its prime objectives was to entice propertied peasants away from the independent Union of Nicaraguan Agricultural Producers (*Union de Productores Agrícolas Nicaragüenses* or UPANIC) and thereby limit potential opposition to the regime. To further this policy, in July 1984 UNAG opened its membership to include rural producers regardless of the size of their landholdings. The union has on occasion favored the distribution of land to peasant households to gain their trust and support; this

policy has generated some conflicts with government officials. Nonetheless, UNAG's chief focus has been to encourage the expansion and consolidation of the cooperative sector. Comandante Tirado has played a central role in
determining UNAG's stance and in selecting dependable
union presidents who are invariably members of the Sandinista Assembly. In fact, all members of UNAG's governing national board are FSLN militants.

To secure organizational control over peasants unwilling to join either the ATC or UNAG, the Sandinistas also
set up the Association of Small and Medium Producers
(*Associación de Pequeños y Medianos Productores* or
APMP). In addition to rallying support for the regime, the
APMP has applied sanctions such as harvest or land seizures against uncooperative peasants who continued selling crops on the private market rather than through state
agencies.[22]

According to Sandinista ideologists, the thousands of
small- and medium-sized rural merchants and storekeepers
will eventually be consigned to the "dustheap of history,"
once the state is able to regulate and oversee the bulk of
domestic trade. The APP has not sufficiently developed,
however, to swallow up small-scale commerce without risk-
ing massive economic destabilization. Most of the population thus remains heavily dependent on private trade as
well as the vast informal economy. Managua is reticent
about comprehensive nationalization of petty retailing
along Soviet and Cuban lines and has largely tolerated an
internal free market while steadily boosting state intervention through price setting and wage controls. The Ministry
of Internal Trade has played an expanding role in regulating
private trade and "contraband exchange" through a network of collection, distribution, and transaction points
around the country. The aim is to establish several hundred
official outlets and "people's foodstores" and gradually sup-
plant the private market. The People's Production Committees (*Comités Populares de Producción* or CPP) were empowered to persuade peasants to sell directly to the state at

specified prices in order to guarantee inexpensive staples to low-income urban residents.

Familiar state socialist marketing problems have appeared in Nicaragua, revolving around official incompetence in collecting, transporting, storing, and distributing produce and manufactured goods. To prevent further deterioration in supplies and encourage output, Managua has in recent years permitted unhindered marketing within departments where state and private purchasing systems often exist side by side. Since the mid-1980s, the prices paid to farmers by the government have been raised, many retail food subsidies have been reduced, and producers have been allowed to sell their crops outside official channels at free market prices. Nonetheless, inter-regional sales continue to be formally restricted to official channels in order to squeeze out the more entrepreneurial middlemen and traders and increase the supplies available to the state.

Land Redistribution

Peasant grievances in many parts of the country were reportedly exacerbated in the early 1980s because of unfulfilled expectations over land redistribution generated by early Sandinista pledges. The popular FSLN slogan "land for the peasants" began to ring increasingly hollow once the regime consolidated its power, imposed an austerity drive, banned unauthorized land seizures, and implemented strict "labor discipline" in various sectors of the economy. Meanwhile, more than 100,000 peasant families continued to subsist on tiny plots or possessed no land at all, thus breeding resentment, suspicion, and opposition to the *Frente*. The regime thus faced what has proved to be a persistent dilemma in its agrarian reforms. On the one hand, by accelerating the expropriation of larger owners and distributing this land to poorer peasants, it would thereby create conflicts with the "patriotic rural bourgeosie," precipitate a fall in the production of agro-experts, and help bolster peasant capitalism. On the other hand, by restricting land redistribution to private homesteads to a bare minimum, it risked exacerbating rifts with peasants not under direct or complete FSLN control.

According to some commentators, the Sandinista leadership has remained divided over agrarian policy, with the more doctrinaire figures favoring state farms, heavy investment in large-scale, capital intensive projects, and a rapid transition to a centralized socialist economy and a proletarianized agriculture. Such a program would involve little or no land distribution to the peasantry.[23] In contrast, the more pragmatic and gradualist comandantes, though sharing their comrades' ultimate objectives, have been willing to accept a slower process of rural socialization and some disbursement of plots to land-hungry peasants in order to maintain stability and productivity during the "national emergency." The "gradualists" or "realists" seem to have carried the day in recent years, but ambiguity remains pronounced in the government's programs. This ambivalence may in fact be deliberate, so as to avoid making long-term commitments to either the larger capitalist farmers or the smaller peasant producers. Indeed, "every pledge to respect the desires of the peasant is coupled to the expectation that the peasantry will evolve to a more socialized consciousness."[24]

In 1980 the Ministry of Agricultural Development was combined with the National Agrarian Reform Institute to form the Ministry of Agricultural Development and Agrarian Reform (MIDINRA) under the control of Comandante Wheelock. Although MIDINRA partly defused pressure from the landless peasants by apportioning land to some 20,000 families between 1981 and 1984, more than 60,000 eligible families received no plots, and the regime continued to favor the creation of the larger cooperative units. In fact, the agrarian reform laws allowed the authorities to reassign land in any organizational form that it chose; hence cooperatives continued to receive the most productive parcels acquired or expropriated from "renegade" landowners.

In 1985 the FSLN decided to make further concessions to assuage *campesino* pressures for land and to prevent rural revolt or a complete loss of the peasantry to the "counterrevolution." An increasing number of large landowners were deemed to be inefficient or undercapitalized producers, and their holdings were appropriated and parceled out to peasants not involved in cooperatives. The latter were required to provide guarantees that the land would be used efficiently. Nevertheless, permanent land ownership was not granted; the new land titles were hedged by various stipulations against inheritance, sale, exchange, and subdivision. Secure and irrevocable land titles, it was argued, would obstruct the future "rationalization" of agriculture and the collectivization of smallholders. The provisional acceptance of familial ownership was officially perceived as merely a "transitory step toward associated forms of production."[25] In addition, no fragmentation of collective or cooperative farms was envisaged, as this would have purportedly assisted the uncontrolled and ultimately undesirable development of "capitalist relations of production" in the countryside.

Cooperatives

Sandinista planners consider the large centralized farms — that is, State Production Units (*Unidad de Producción Estatal* or UPE) — to be the driving force of agricultural accumulation. They cover about 20 percent of all cultivable land in the country and are commonly located in the most fertile regions. The UPEs numbered about 1,500 in 1982 and 2,200 in 1985. They were subsequently consolidated into 170 regional state complexes (*Complejos Agrícolas*) administered by MIDINRA appointees (heirs of the Somoza foremen or *mandadores*) and the local "production consultative councils."[26] The 27 state agricultural enterprises (*Empresas Agrícolas*) confiscated from Somoza, including slaughter houses, packing concerns, and food processing plants, were placed under the management of a subdivision of MIDINRA.

The UPEs initially proved to be more productive than Soviet-type state and collective farms because the Sandinistas had simply appropriated the most efficient *latifundios*. But production difficulties began to surface after only one growing season. They stemmed from incompetent management, uncontrolled operating costs, overemployment, organizational inefficiency, resource squandering, worker disincentive, apathy, neglect, and abandonment of these units by skilled technicians in search of better pay, conditions, and prospects in the private sector.

The government has sought ways to reduce expenditure in the UPEs by cutting back on credits and employment, controlling wage increases, and limiting the growth of social services. Overall, such measures have not greatly affected productivity, and state farm accounts tellingly remain one of the most closely guarded secrets in Nicaragua. In the estimation of some outside researchers sympathetic to the FSLN, even though state farms receive about one quarter of all agricultural credits, they only produce approximately one-eighth of the total value of produce.[27]

Officials also admit that *campesinos* have proved to be less than enthusiastic about employment on state farms.[28] The UPEs were reportedly alien, alienating, and lacking in material motivators in comparison to private farming. Workers on state units resented the intensive levels of ideological indoctrination and "political involvement" required by FSLN and ATC cadres through incessant mass meetings and rallies, compulsory security duties, and repetitive educational classes. These sessions and obligations were also a drain on time and labor, while the actual input of rural workers into managerial decision making remained nominal and cosmetic.

In addition to constructing large state farms, the Sandinistas have encouraged the transition toward peasant cooperatives primarily through economic pressures and persuasion rather than direct physical compulsion. Most evidence indicates that force has only been selectively applied against particularly obstinate peasants. The ATC and other mass associations proved to be useful vehicles for mobilizing *campesinos* and organizing rural cooperatives. In sum, about 2,500 cooperative units were formed by mid-1980 and some 3,200 by the close of 1982; by 1984, about 15 percent of all arable land had been collectivized. Of the total amount of land confiscated and redistributed, aside from the UPEs, about 83 percent was earmarked for the cooperatives and only 17 percent for individual farmers; more than 13,000 peasant families were organized into cooperatives by 1983.[29] Peasant access to land and credits often depended on their willingness to join or establish cooperatives. Outright opposition to socialization could sometimes presage severe material hardship for the household in question.

In stark contrast to the official cooperative campaign, private sector attempts to promote agrarian cooperatives have been viewed by the regime as a threat that could seriously diminish the impact of FSLN-sponsored collectives. The Sandinistas attacked as "counterrevolutionary" all cooperatives among small farmers that were funded by private business organizations and in which peasants obtained an individual stake in profit sharing and co-ownership.[30] The authorities have been less willing to provide credit incentives to the small number of private sector cooperatives that apparently promote "other political agendas" than those of the official farms. Evidently the regime has not been seeking an independent cooperative sector but a politically supervised agrarian stratum aiding the advance of socialism. Nonetheless, the agrarian labor force reportedly prefers to labor in the remaining autonomous cooperative enterprises in which material incentives are higher and blatant political manipulation is absent.

Sandinista propaganda has depicted state-sponsored cooperativism as a spontaneous "indigenous movement" previously stifled by capitalist or "precapitalist" production relations but successfully liberated by the revolution. In fact, rural socialization in Nicaragua can only be visualized as voluntary if one discounts the economic pressures applied by the regime against the expansion of private farming and if one ignores official stipulations that favor collectives in the allocation of credits, machinery, fertilizer, pesticides, and animal feed.[31] Black describes how some large farms have been nationalized or organized into cooperatives to create the impression of peasant spontaneity. FSLN agitators among the work force call a strike claiming "capitalist exploitation" or "economic sabotage" by the owners. The authorities then formally intervene in the dispute to adjudicate between the owner and his work force and invariably decide to socialize the farm because of "popular pressure." Although peasant self-reliance has been deliberately curtailed through limitations on technical and financial assistance, cooperative farms, despite their persistent economic shortcomings, have received a growing share of state subsidies to encourage peasant enlistment. In such cases, ensuring political control over the rural population has evidently taken precedence over questions of sheer economic rationality and productivity for the *Frente*.

Two kinds of cooperatives have been created to facilitate FSLN supervision and more thorough state intervention in the production of basic foodstuffs. These are the Credit and Service Cooperatives (*Cooperativa de Credito y Servicio* or CCS) and the Sandinista Agricultural Cooperatives (*Cooperativa Agrícola Sandinista* or CAS). The two forms are not in competition but are viewed as sequential stages of economic organization that gradually introduce "socialist relations of production" in the peasant economy. In the "lower level," CCS technical assets and credits are socialized or pooled, but land remains individually held by small- and medium-sized owners. Members of a CCS can select the varieties of crops cultivated on their plots, but their affiliation with the cooperative involves "collective administration of government assistance in production and marketing . . . participation in farm-wide patterns of labor exchange, the use of collectively owned inputs and implements, and attendance at . . . political education and 'study circles.'"[32] CCS participants sell their produce through ENABAS, the state marketing agency, which guarantees regulated prices for a variety of staple crops and helps subsidize the consumer prices of foodstuffs. CCS arrangements have become more prevalent among the middle and upper peasantry, where wholesale confiscation might have ignited concerted opposition and led to a marked drop in yields. The CCS cooperatives claimed 48,712 members combined in 397 farms by 1985, with each unit containing some 25 to 35 peasant households.[33]

The CAS collectives are officially regarded as "more advanced forms of socialization" in which members are required to pool all of their resources, collectively "own" the land, contribute labor according to predetermined production norms, and evenly divide essential food and goods. Each cooperative is administered by a *Junta Directiva*, which coordinates production schedules and assigns work to the labor force. All CAS income is controlled by the management and allocated to cover operating costs, social services, capital investments, and member earnings. Wage payments are distributed according to the amount of collective labor contributed by each individual or household during a set period of time.

The CAS collectives initially formed a very small sector of the agrarian economy, encompassing only 1.3 percent of the arable land and mostly incorporating poor peasants and rural workers who had been subjected to a prolonged period of political work by FSLN cadres.[34] During the early 1980s these "advanced" units grew to incorporate over one-third of all agricultural cooperatives and have steadily expanded ever since. By 1986 about 28 percent of all cultivable land had been assigned to cooperatives, with the CAS gradually predominating. Managua claimed the existence of nearly 4,000 cooperatives by 1984, involving more than half of all peasant producers, or around 60,000 *campesinos*.[35]

The Sandinistas have also established "mixed cooperatives" or "pre-cooperatives" as halfway points between the

CCS and the CAS. In these farms, "collective ownership" of land exists alongside familial management of smaller plots within the cooperative. The government has also encouraged temporary "work collectives" for the duration of a growing season or focused on gathering a particular harvest.

One important function of the various cooperatives has been to hold people in the countryside and stem the mass migrations to urban areas, particularly to the capital, which have overloaded the cities' creaking infrastructure.[36] The flight to the cities has evidently increased the size of the "nonproductive" population immersed in the informal economy. This urban influx has not contributed to any notable expansion of the industrial proletariat, especially as the regime does not have sufficient investment funds available to enlarge Nicaragua's industrial sector.

The rural cooperatives obtained most of the land distributed by the state after 1981 as well as an increasing proportion of credits and supplies. The CAS is more common among the poorer peasantry and semi-proletarians, whose economic and political manipulation has generally proved easier to enforce. The regime purportedly plans to expand the cooperative sector gradually in line with its projected political objectives. Despite declining rates of productivity in many cooperatives, the FSLN has continued to broaden the range of material resources available for their formation and maintenance. In contrast to the steady growth in agrarian collectives, urban cooperatives have only registered modest success thus far among small-scale artisans. By 1983 about 4,600 workshops had been organized into 77 "service cooperatives" while 15 state production collectives were established for the industrial work force.[37]

The authorities reportedly remain "confident of the superior results of associated production" over individualized farming in the long term despite strong indicators to the contrary, especially from the grossly inefficient CAS.[38] In addition to pronounced economic setbacks the *Frente* has faced persistent peasant opposition to induced collectivization, manifested in a reluctance to join, lack of labor discipline, consistently low productivity, and passive resistance or indifference to political indoctrination. In stark economic terms and contrary to expectations, the official cooperatives have neither reduced production costs in agriculture nor raised incomes and living standards for the *campesinos*. Indeed, net purchasing power among collectivized peasants has steadily decreased since the Sandinista takeover.

Agrarian Problems

The economic malaise that has gripped Nicaragua since the turn of the decade has been caused by a combination of internal and external factors.[39] They include the initial civil war devastation; a critical foreign exchange situation, including a large overseas debt; the costly post-Somoza reconstruction program; the state's extension of social services; the wider economic crisis in Latin America, involving falling export prices and rising import costs; the U.S. trade embargo and restrictions on technology exports; the diversion of national income to defense, militarization, and the "contra war"; mismanagement by managerially inexperienced political appointees; erratic state economic policies; and decreasing investment by the private sector, which remains concerned about future government policies.

Irrespective of government claims, the contra war and the U.S. embargo are clearly insufficient in themselves to account for the severe economic decline in which the country's gross domestic product contracted by 11.6 percent between 1980 and 1985. During this time a great deal of foreign development aid has been forthcoming from Western Europe and Latin America, while the areas in which the bulk of armed combat has occurred are not critical to the economy. Most of the country's GNP is actually generated in the relatively tranquil Pacific coast regions. Although coffee exporting has been hurt by the conflict in the highland regions, the production of sugar, for example, in an area largely unaffected by the civil war has plummeted to about three-quarters of what it was in 1978. Although the national population increased by about 20 percent between 1979 and 1985, food output and the domestic grain supply have been shrinking. Declining yields can be principally blamed on incompetent administration and coordination in the state and cooperative sectors, as well as on the disincentives for increasing output in the private sector. In addition, the authorities have diverted foodstocks to help supply their growing military machine and security apparatus and have stockpiled some staples for possible future emergencies.

Contrary to FSLN propaganda, the poorest stratum of farmers and rural semi-proletarians has suffered an absolute drop in living standards because of high inflation, infrastructural breakdown, and overall economic decline. David Kaimowitz believes that these people often face the greatest shortages because

> they have no connections with the organized distribution mechanisms of the cities, do not have access to the commissaries made available to the permanent workers on the large farms, and have neither the buying power nor transportation facilites that have allowed other producers to gain access to the market. Private merchants who have in the past offered them consumer items, albeit at monopoly prices, have been eliminated and the government does not have the capacity to replace them.[40]

According to observers,

> Increased worker productivity in rural areas largely depends on both favorable agricultural prices as well as on the ability of the industrial sector and, hence, urban workers to supply increased supplies of manufactured goods. . . . If this is not met through increased domestic production of manufactured goods and imports, it is unlikely that increases in labor productivity in agriculture can be realized.[41]

Deterioration in food production and exports has reduced foreign exchange earnings, lowered imports, and aggravated the shortage of practically all items, thus decreasing incomes and living standards among all sectors of society.[42] The export of agricultural produce to earn foreign currency and to meet Soviet bloc obligations has also contributed to the scarcity of various essential foods. Despite these shipments, Nicaragua has a large external trade deficit because of its poor performance in the export sector, especially with the decline in world market demands for its traditional agricultural exports. Deteriorating trade relations have increased dependence on foreign assistance and credits and raised the national debt to over $5 billion.

The cumulative effects of inflation and resource scarcity have evidently hit peasants and agricultural workers very hard. With runaway inflation since the mid-1980s and the plummeting value of domestic currency, many Nicaraguans without ready access to dollars have reverted to a virtual barter economy, using food and other items to conduct their transactions. Various degrees of "revolutionary austerity" have been imposed by Managua throughout the last decade to maintain some economic equilibrium with the reduction of consumer subsidies and the rationing of many basic goods. The most recent austerity package introduced in January 1989 involved sharp cutbacks in government food subsidies and investments. This package will undoubtedly increase rural and urban unemployment and result in a further degeneration in public services and living standards.

Forrest Colburn demonstrates how the regime's agrarian policies, which are ostensibly designed to improve conditions among the rural poor, are actually subordinate to wider economic and political programs and have severely undermined the welfare of all citizens.[43] Even some pro-Sandinista sympathizers concede that "the policy of fixing price relationships between agriculture and industry, and between agro-export production and production for the domestic market, combined with the imbalance in supply mechanisms in the countryside, discriminated against the peasantry."[44] *Campesinos* increasingly assert that they are worse off than they were before the revolution. Hence, the government has lost substantial support among some of the very people it avowedly wanted to help most. The FSLN has evidently been more concerned to ensure the survival of the regime and the well-being of its cadres and urban support base than to improve the welfare of the peasantry and other rural sectors. Economic shortages and rationing have of course also been manipulated by the Sandinistas to extend their controls over the population and to enmesh large sectors of the populace in a dependency relationship with the state and its various agencies.

With growing internal turmoil in much of the Communist world over questions of economic organization and the role of the peasantry and the agrarian work force, it remains to be seen what adjustments Managua will make to its as yet incomplete socialist transformation. The majority of entrenched Leninist regimes eradicated private enterprise at an early stage in their consolidation of power. Many are now seeking ways of reintroducing market elements and incentive schemes to stimulate economic recovery without surrendering the party's overall political control. By contrast, Nicaragua has maintained a sizable private sector, estimated to cover about two thirds of the economy, even while strictly curbing its political impact. Theoretically, it may therefore find it easier than other Communist states to stimulate production by encouraging the remaining private proprietors. This may be accomplished through various legal guarantees over land ownership, more favorable pricing and taxation policies, and allowances for the expansion of free markets.

On the other hand, the severity of the economic crisis and the persistence of private interest groups and opposition forces could hypothetically have the reverse effect on FSLN policies. Managua may find it expedient to crack down more harshly in the future on independent groupings and even seek to impose a "war economy." More thorough state controls would serve to prevent the growth of organized opposition and stymie the threat of destabilization and widespread social unrest.

How economic recovery can be reconciled with political repression is a more immediate concern for the regime. In the long term, however, the Sandinistas confront even more daunting contradictions – between their Communist polity and the semi-socialized economy, as well as between their planned "transition to socialism" and the imperative of avoiding further economic decline and political disruption. In recent months, Sandinista officials have announced proposals for a "new deal" with the private sector, including preparations for an updated law on land reform and security of tenure.[45] Such legislation would evidently guarantee greater government respect for private property and purportedly make the "mixed economy" a more permanent feature of the economic landscape rather than a mere "transitional phase." It remains unclear, however, whether such legalistic stipulations will be sufficient to stimulate output, reassure farmers, and attract investors, or how far in practice they will curtail state interference in production and marketing.

4

Sandinista Policies:
Indigenous Peoples

Relations between the Sandinistas and the indigenous population of Nicaragua's Atlantic Coast region highlight some key issues concerning the plight of ethnic minorities under revolutionary Communist regimes. An examination of government policies toward indigenous minorities also helps broaden the picture of rural transformations instigated by the FSLN since its seizure of power. In standard Latin American usage, the term *indigenas* refers to communities that maintain a distinct native language and preserve some elements of pre-Hispanic culture, regardless of their precise ethnic background. About 6 percent of Nicaragua's population maintains a separate non-*ladino* identity, including the Miskito, Sumu, and Rama Indians descended from the pre-Columbian indigenous people, and the black Creoles and Caribs (Garifunas), whose racial background includes admixtures of African, Amerindian, and European.[1]

The Indian, Creole, and Carib societies principally inhabit the department of Zelaya in eastern Nicaragua, particularly its coastal and riverine areas.[2] According to figures compiled in the mid-1970s, Indians represent 4 percent of the national population, blacks (Creoles and Caribs) form 9 percent, "whites" about 17 percent, and *mestizos* (those of mixed Hispanic and Indian blood who retain few, if any, indigenous cultural traits) roughly 70 percent.[3] Approximately 9 percent of Nicaraguans live in Zelaya, which forms almost half of the national territory.

According to recent estimates the Miskitos number around 120,000 dispersed in over 200 communities; in the northeastern section of the department they constitute a majority.[4] Between 5,000 and 9,000 Sumu Indians live in about 30 villages in the northern interior regions of Zelaya. The Rama number under 1,000 and reside in a handful of settlements along the southeast coast. Around 30,000 black Creoles and 1,500 Caribs also inhabit the southern coastal regions, concentrated in and around the town of Bluefields (Creoles) and Pearl Lagoon (Caribs). All non-Hispanic minorities total nearly 40 percent of the Zelayan population. The rest of the *costeños* (Atlantic Coast residents) are *mestizos*, most of whom migrated to the area since the 1950s. They number over 185,000 and live mostly in the western, southern, and south central areas.

The exact total of the indigenous populace is difficult to ascertain and varies considerably according to different sources. Interestingly enough, the statistics made available in December 1981 by the Research and Documentation Center of the Atlantic Coast (*Centro de Investigación y Documentación de la Costa Atlántica* or CIDCA), a research unit for the FSLN's Ministry for the Atlantic Coast (*Ministerio de Costa Atlántica* or MICA), show a significantly smaller Indian population (under 100,000) than the figures often cited by nongovernmental sources. In contrast, unofficial estimates compiled by Nicaragua's independent Indian organizations sometimes raise the figure to nearly 170,000. The discrepancies may be partly due to the use of different criteria for defining Indian identity, as well as the result of deliberate political maneuvering by the protagonists in the east coast conflict.

Historical Background

The Atlantic Coast Indians were largely spared from the ravages of conquest and colonization since the sixteenth century, as the eastern side of the isthmus was not greatly valued by Iberian settlers. Indian communities survived with a high degree of internal cohesion and autonomy.[5] Of the two smaller groups, the Rama were formerly distributed as far south as Costa Rica, but lost much of their homelands during the eighteenth and nineteenth centuries as a result of Miskito territorial expansion.[6] The Sumu habitat was also more extensive before Spanish and Miskito encroachments; indeed the term "Sumu" is a nineteenth century designation for all interior Indian tribes of Nicaragua. Unlike the Miskitos the Sumu and Rama avoided mixed marriages with settlers and traders; this contributed to reducing their population over the centuries.[7]

The term "Miskito" appeared during the 1600s as a label applied by English buccaneers to the coastal tribes. The Miskitos themselves can be divided into three major groups corresponding to their location, dialect, and cultural variations – the coastal, riverine, and Honduran (Mam) groups. According to anthropologist Mary Helms, the Miskitos are a racially mixed Amerindian–Afro-American "colonial tribe" that has retained its "Indian" identity.[8] They successfully adjusted to their limited colonial experience by adopting new economic pursuits, developing advantageous trading relations with outsiders, and integrating black and white immigrants. The newcomers tended to assimilate Indian cultural practices, social features, and economic patterns.

Pre-contact Miskito subsistence was based on swiddening (crop rotation), hunting, fishing, and local trading. English buccaneers established mutually beneficial relations with the coastal Indians. They were not interested in permanent settlement but enlisted Miskitos in sea and land conflicts with the Spaniards and provided them with European artifacts in return.[9] By the end of the eighteenth century, the Miskitos gained ascendancy over other Indian groups between the present Honduran and Costa Rican borders. They were aided by the acquisition of guns and valuable trading items from the English and increasingly adopted a middleman role between interior tribes and the Europeans. Helms defines the Miskitos as a "purchase society" in which internal political autonomy and a stable social organization were maintained while economic networks were developed with the outside world.[10] By incorporating European goods they strengthened their resilience to cultural, military, and political penetration. By absorbing outsiders they maintained or steadily increased their numbers.

After the demise of piracy, the British Crown increasingly viewed the Miskito coast as an ideal base for its Caribbean operations. The alliance forged with the Indians in the seventeenth century proved strategically important by keeping Spain confined to western Nicaragua. The Miskitos in turn benefited from English protection against Hispanic encroachments. From 1661 to 1894, the Miskitos were symbolically ruled by 15 kings sponsored by London to counter Spanish claims to *Mosquitia*.[11] Though kingship became a focus of Miskito identity vis-à-vis outsiders and for official dealings with the British, the office exerted little internal political authority.

During the nineteenth century the Indians were evangelized by Moravian Protestant missionaries who eventually displaced indigenous rituals and beliefs and contributed significant health care and educational benefits. The Moravian faith became a virtual national religion for the Miskitos; it also promoted greater Indian cultural uniformity and more stable village settlements based around Moravian chapels. The pastors began to play an important role in community affairs as moral advisers and dispute resolvers. The Miskitos' British-Caribbean orientation, their Protestantism, and a deeply rooted mistrust of the Nicaraguan "Spaniards" set the tone for their negative perception of later *ladino* influences and their conflicts with the Sandinistas.

Like the Miskitos, Nicaragua's Creoles are culturally closer to the English-speaking Caribbean than to Central America's *ladinos*. The Creoles migrated from various Caribbean islands during the seventeenth century and initially worked on the southern coastal plantations. A sector of the community eventually took up positions as merchants, small entrepreneurs, local administrators, and

Moravian pastors.[12] Since the nineteenth century, the Creole population has spread northward; although remaining more urban-based than the Indians, it provided an important point of contact between Amerindian and Anglo-Caribbean culture.

The Garifunas were a mix of Carib Indians and fugitive African slaves who were deported to the mainland by the British and migrated to Nicaragua in the late 1800s.[13] They settled in a small area of the southeast coast, where they divided their subsistence pursuits between agriculture, trading, and laboring in coastal towns for national and foreign companies.

Nicaragua obtained independence from Spain in 1821. The British were gradually pushed out of the Atlantic Coast region, and a semi-autonomous "Miskito reserve" was created. Under the 1860 Treaty of Managua, London recognized Nicaraguan claims to the area, but the agreement also specified that "the Miskito Indians within the district shall enjoy the right of governing according to their own customs and . . . the Republic of Nicaragua agrees to respect and not to interfere with such customs and regulations. . . . "[14]

In 1877, Miskito leaders rejected proposals for integration as a province of Nicaragua, which led to the successful military campaign by President General José Santos Zelaya. Under the pretext of "reincorporation," Managua occupied the coastal areas, deposed the Miskito king, and pressured Indian leaders to sign a declaration of allegiance, thus establishing at least nominal central control over Indian lands. Zelaya allowed for the entry of U.S. companies to bring capital and employment to the local inhabitants. The Miskito in turn welcomed U.S. corporations as a counterbalance to Hispanization. By the turn of the century, Indians had become increasingly reliant on wage labor with foreign-owned mining and lumbering concerns and banana and coconut plantations.[15] Although Indian dependence on imported foods and goods expanded, Western companies did not interfere greatly with traditional community life or with Indian political autonomy.

Throughout their history of contact with outsiders, "the adaptability of the Miskitos' traditional indigenous subsistence system has enabled them to participate in two worlds: their own kin-based, reciprocal exchange, subsistence society and the foreign wage labor and money market economy."[16] Indian involvement with foreign companies during this century has been characterized by repeated "boom and bust" cycles to which they responded by interjecting seasonal wage labor into their economic patterns.[17] With increasing economic dependence on foreign markets, by the 1970s Miskito economic diversification became a "response to decline of security of livelihood within villages rather than an adaptation to maximize external opportunities."[18]

Despite a more pronounced reliance on external markets, under the Somoza dynasty, the Indian population was for the most part ignored and neglected by the government. Aside from control over mining and fishing enterprises, Managua sought little direct political domination and provided only minimal economic assistance to Zelaya department. As a result, the Indians and Creoles neither supported the Somozas nor harbored any great resentment against them. The indigenous people were only sporadically involved in any revolutionary activity against the dictatorship.[19]

During the 1920s and 1930s, Indian experience with Augusto Sandino along the Río Coco and in the northeast regions was largely negative.[20] Sandino's forces attacked major coastal lumber and banana companies in their campaign against the U.S. presence. The destruction or closure of these concerns destroyed employment for thousands of Indian workers and local tradesmen who did not consider themselves exploited or oppressed by foreign corporations. Moreover, Sandino's guerrillas confiscated food and property in many areas of operation and intimidated uncooperative communities. This fanned friction and resentment, reduced *costeño* sympathy for the initial rebel cause, and bred ambivalence about the subsequent Sandinista insurgency. FSLN officials admit that the "anti-imperialist struggle" of

Sandino and the *Frente* was "misunderstood" and not supported by the majority of Indians and Creoles. Somoza's propaganda against the FSLN also helped promote the image of the rebels as mere bandits and atheists. Conversely, Sandinista perceptions of the indigenous people were clouded by the notion that Miskitos and Creoles were widely recruited into the National Guard.

Before the Communist takeover, the Atlantic Coast populations exercised substantial local self-rule, cultural and religious independence, and a high degree of subsistence autonomy outside the areas confiscated from Indians by Somoza's Institute for National Development. Managuan and foreign companies did not generally interfere in internal Indian affairs and failed to generate long-term economic opportunities for the natives. The Somoza regime established police stations in several larger towns to maintain law and order, and village headmen were answerable to local Somoza officials; but no military service was required of Indians, no taxes were imposed on land and personal property, and no major integrationist plans or disruptive development schemes were pursued. During the popular insurrection and overthrow of *Somocismo*, the Indian and Creole areas witnessed little or no fighting, as few FSLN units were active in the region. The indigenous people displayed little enthusiasm either for the Somoza dictatorship or for the Sandinista cause. The *Frente* lacked any grassroots organizations or firm bases of support to help build their networks of social and political control in the region.

Ideology and Ethnic Policies

An evaluation of the early stages of the Sandinista regime in the Indian and Creole areas requires that the ideological dimensions of the FSLN's minorities program be examined. The Miskito, Sumu, and Rama traditionally occupied a low social and cultural status in the *ladino* worldview. For centuries *ladinos* have assumed an ostensible cultural superiority toward the native peoples. FSLN cadres have not been immune to such ethnocentric prejudices and indeed have blended them with their own peculiar ideological preconceptions. In Sandinista theory, traditional Amerindian societies are an impediment to "historical progress" and economic development. The indigenous peoples must therefore be drawn into the larger Nicaraguan political system and class structure, essentially as peasants and workers.[21] Their ethnic specificity has been attacked as "reactionary," with Indians viewed as ideologically retarded, culturally backward, and possessing a "primitive social organization." According to Marxist theorists, these attributes are not necessarily the result of some innate racial or ethnic characteristics but a consequence of centuries of colonialism. Imperialist interference allegedly kept the natives imprisoned in an essentially "precapitalist mode of production," thus blocking the progressive development of social classes.[22]

From the outset, the Sandinistas stressed their "anti-imperialist" mission in the coastal areas, which were purportedly permeated by a regressive "pro-Western" mentality. Indian, Creole, and Garifuna societies were denied any authentic or separate "national identity" by FSLN policy makers. The FSLN argument that British and American imperialism had "robbed them [the indigenous tribes] of their identity" became a useful pretext for the Sandinistas' version of "national integration." Native claims to self-determination have been consistently dismissed as "indigenism," purportedly a product of imperialism that has in the past prevented full Nicaraguan unity. To justify further their "revolutionary transformations" and anti-autonomy policies on the Atlantic Coast, the comandantes have also used "breakthrough historical materialism" to prove that the Miskitos themselves were formerly "oppressors and slave owners" of other Indian groups.[23]

Government officials have admitted a lack of respect or "insensitivity" among Sandinista cadres toward Indian customs. Much of this "disrespect" was due to a combination of deeply rooted racism, political indoctrination, and ideological self-righteousness, which asserted that indigenous societies were subordinate to a "higher revolutionary goal." Indian leaders have repeatedly accused the regime of anti-Indian and anti-black racism and a thinly veiled neocolonialism. Even keen Sandinista supporters concede that the *compañeros* (comrades) brought their prejudices to the Coast:

> For the first Sandinista "missionaries" the Atlantic Coast people were primitive, backward in all respects. Their cultural and religious practices were often ridiculed and depreciated. Like most missionaries, the Sandinistas assumed a blank page of primitivism that needed to be written on by modern civilization.[24]

In many instances, latent racism displayed by the *ladino* cadres has itself been used as an excuse by the regime for its mistreatment of native peoples. By presenting such racism as a remnant of capitalism and colonialism that the FSLN is intent on eradicating, the regime obscures the paternalistic bias in its own ethnic policies. Conversely, the Indians themselves have been deliberately accused of racist prejudices toward the "Spaniards" to help justify government intervention. Managua's claim, for example, that Miskito leaders sought to expel the *ladino* peasantry from the region served to legitimate stricter central control as a necessary measure to prevent potential ethnic conflicts. Thus, the Sandinistas could pose both as protectors of the *campesinos* and as important arbiters in Indian-*ladino* disputes.

FSLN soldiers and administrators were allowed great leeway in their treatment of native peoples, particularly in the early stages of political centralization. This allowed substantial scope for individual and collective abuses; according to *Frente* spokesmen, "overenthusiastic help" coupled with a "limited knowledge of the region's history" inadvertently destroyed some "important traditions" that were in any case "objectively" doomed. Sandinista leaders envisaged all political and social problems as essentially "class-based"; hence, the ethnic minority question was conceived primarily in economic determinist terms. The goal was to rearrange subsistence patterns, political structures, and class relations to further "socialist development." In the long run, with the construction of socialism and the elimination of antagonistic classes the revolutionary administration would avowedly also "eliminate the fundamental causes of racism and ethnocentrism."[25]

In stark contrast, for Indian groups self-determination and the autonomy of *Wan Tasbaia* (Our Land) were the central issues, while the building of a "new Nicaragua" according to Sandinista prescriptions was a secondary concern: "In direct contrast, the *costeños*, above all the Miskitos, saw things in an almost wholly ethnonational terms. For them the problem was the *mestizo*-dominated Managuan government that was trying to reorient their way of living."[26] Indian rights to self-rule and land ownership were denied by Managua because "the validity of the demands of an ethnic group ultimately have to be judged by their class content."[27] In other words, the *Frente* leadership was empowered to decide which community could receive any modicum of autonomy as well as the precise form and content of native self-determination. The Indians were to downplay their ethnic identity, consider themselves as "poor *campesinos*," and thus be brought into the mainstream of the Sandinista regime. To further this process, the FSLN combated the independent Indian organization, the Alliance for the Progress of the Miskitos and Sumus (*Alianza Para el Progreso de los Miskitos y Sumu* or ALPROMISU), which campaigned for greater local control over land, resources, and political institutions.

ALPROMISU was founded in 1972 by Indian leaders to promote Indian identity, control communal property, sponsor development projects, and work for cultural revitalization. It had ties to the World Council of Indigenous Peoples and the World Council of Churches, where it gained international sympathy for the plight of Nicaragua's Amerindians. A similar organization, the National Association of Sumu Communities (*Sumu Kalpa Pakna Waingre Lane* or SUKAWALA) was created among the Sumu in 1979, but its activities were more restricted than ALPROMISU's. SUKAWALA was officially reactivated in mid-1985 under firm FSLN supervision. ALPROMISU, which encountered some repression and manipulation under Somoza, was initially encouraged by the Sandinista takeover and put forward its own plans for reclaiming and expanding native rights. The FSLN became alarmed by the resurgence of Indian demands, dismissed many of them as "politically retrograde," and proceeded to undermine the ALPROMISU movement and its democratically elected leadership.[28]

Native autonomy claims were labeled "separatist," purportedly aimed at "dismantling Nicaragua" because they conflicted with the FSLN's integrationist blueprints. Under the influence and direction of "foreign agencies," some local leaders were supposedly plotting to "restore imperialist domination" in the region. According to the *Frente*, the choice for Indians was not between self-rule and subjugation to Managuan *dictat*, but between an "alliance with foreign interests" and "unity with the Nicaraguan nation." The former option would avowedly place the indigenous peoples under officially unacceptable U.S. control.[29] Native independence movements were therefore denounced as "counterrevolutionary" and in basic conflict with the "historic and revolutionary interests" of the country's Indians and Creoles.

An additional pretext for limiting Indian self-rule revolved around the threat of outside intervention by "counterrevolutionary" (contra) forces, which were ostensibly exploiting separatist demands to promote internal strife.[30] In fact the native leaders were neither colluding with the embryonic contra movement nor seeking outright secession from Nicaragua. They were soliciting a bilateral agreement with the central authorities guaranteeing traditional forms of self-government and respect for local land claims within an overarching single state structure. Despite their nonseparatist quest, the indigenous peoples were from the beginning earmarked for incorporation in the emerging party-state system as subjects of the Sandinista-directed process of development. Nicaragua was officially declared "unitary and indivisible," irrespective of any concessions to "cultural autonomy." In the heated words of the foremost academic authority on the country's Indians, "The Sandinista state's invasion, occupation, confiscation, and repression are but racist and supremacist brutalities unleashed by many Third World States – the new colonialists – against indigenous nations."[31]

Consolidation of Central Control

The FSLN's "Historic Program" of 1969 declared that the Atlantic Coast regions had been totally neglected and kept docile under Somoza and effectively divorced from the nation. Once in power, the *Frente* underscored that the indigenous "isolated multi-ethnic population had little concept of the role of a central government."[32] Under the slogans of "reincorporation" and "national development," Managua proceeded to place the department of Zelaya under tighter political and economic control. The Nicaraguan Institute for Natural Resources and the Environment (*Instituto Nicaragüense de Recursos Naturales y del Ambiente* or IRENA) was authorized to oversee and direct the development of east coast resources, and the Ministry for the Atlantic Coast (MICA) was created to plan more closely the region's economic projects and social mobilization schemes. The Nicaraguan Institute for the Atlantic Coast (*Instituto Nicaragüense de la Costa Atlántica* or INICA) and the Research and Documentation Center of the Atlantic Coast (CIDCA) were formed to help coordinate and monitor the process. In mid-1982 INICA was replaced by a regional government system with military governors assigned for the northern and southern sections of Zelaya.

Through their program of "revolutionary integration,"

the Sandinistas were intent on destroying indigenous sources of authority and all independent organizations in the Indian and Creole communities. The Indian village-based elders' councils and other local bodies were rejected as unprogressive and replaced by the CDS and various mass organizations usually staffed by politically reliable *ladino* cadres. One key mass association was established in November 1979 in place of the disbanded ALPROMISU. It was styled as Miskito, Sumu, Rama, Sandinista Unity (*Miskitu Sumu Rama Sandinista Asla Takanka* or MISURASATA) and groomed to transform "ethnic groups" into fully fledged Nicaraguan "new people." MISURASATA was designed to function as a standard FSLN mass body and was provided with a token seat in the Council of State. The association soon began to gain some genuine grassroots support, however. Ironically, with the formation of MISURASATA, the FSLN helped to stimulate a new national awakening among the Miskitos, and the regime itself became the major target of Indian criticisms and eventual rebellion.[33]

In their "Plan of Action for 1981," MISURASATA leaders put forward more coherent demands for self-determination. They also sponsored organizational pluralism for coastal workers, youth, women, and other social categories, thus countering Managua's efforts at centralization modeled on its Pacific Coast program. As a result of its independent orientation, MISURASATA became the object of mounting government attacks, and its policies were denigrated as subversive secessionism and "indigent agitation."[34]

The Sandinistas feared the growing influence of the MISURASATA leadership and were determined to prevent the emergence of a strong alternative source of authority in the indigenous areas. The formal structures of MISURASATA were dissolved by government decree in early 1981 after the arrest of 33 leaders, including its directorate and nearly every community level activist. They were accused of sowing "Indianism" and "counterrevolution" and of plotting to establish a separate Indian government. The arrests came before the MISURASATA leadership could formally resign from the Council of State as a protest against increasingly repressive government policies. Other prominent native leaders were either imprisoned, forced into exile, politically neutralized, or murdered; some also fled the country or went into hiding. The Organization of American States (OAS) concluded that "hundreds of Miskitos have been arbitrarily detained without any formalities and under vague accusations of carrying out 'counterrevolutionary activities.'"[35]

Sandinization proceeded apace throughout the 1980s as new government agencies proliferated and heightened political and military control over the region. MISURASATA sympathizers were removed from any decision-making role on local councils; only closely scrutinized FSLN appointees could henceforth hold office. The regime also brought in trusted people from outside the region to assume positions in local administration, thus aiming to prevent community solidarity and concerted opposition to the central government.[36] The *Frente's* "divide and rule" strategy, fashioned to restrict intra- and inter-ethnic cooperation, also involved the formation of separate organizations for the Sumu and Creoles and the promotion of a few reliable natives to nominally high positions in local state institutions. As most Indians were considered politically untrustworthy by the FSLN, "westerners" and *ladino* locals were often favored in obtaining government employment. Sandinista spokesmen have confirmed the marginal participation of coastal people in the "economic and political insitutions of the revolutionary government during the early years."[37]

Indian resistance to official manipulation and co-optation proved resilient among both ordinary villagers and the educated "elite," who evaded incorporation in the FSLN's political structures and emerged as the "backbone of the Miskito contra movement."[38] Sandinista policies provoked demonstrations, passive opposition, and noncooperation; they also aroused the growth of armed Indian resistance discussed in the next chapter.

Managua similarly sought to place the Creole and Garifuna populations under stiffer central control. It refused to
recognize the Southern Indigenous Creole Community
(SICC) organization, jailed its leaders, and commenced sup-
planting it with Sandinista-supervised associations. The
importing of loyalist administrators, *ladino* "technicians,"
as well as Cuban "advisers" and "teachers," into Creole and
Indian areas led to local accusations of providing "jobs to
foreign communists" in a region suffering acute unemployment.[39] The Creoles' "English language, taken together with
their British Empire antecedents, seemed to make them
obvious, imperial, stereotypical targets for a collectivist-
inclined revolutionary regime."[40] Creole predominance in the
Zelayan "petite bourgeoisie" and the Moravian Church also
earned them a "capitalist-imperialist" label from the FSLN.
They have also been frequently charged as "anti-Communist" because of their attachment to the English-speaking
Caribbean and to North America.

Political Indoctrination and State Control

As in the rest of Nicaragua, the FSLN launched a mass
indoctrination campaign in Indian and Creole areas after
assuming control over all educational and social service programs. The literacy drives in Indian communities were designed to help break down cultural and linguistic barriers
between Miskitos and *ladinos* and facilitate Sandinista
schooling. Approximately 50 percent of Indians in northeast Zelaya evidently spoke little or no Spanish when the
FSLN took over, thus making it difficult to sustain official
indoctrination. The first two "literacy crusades" conducted
in Spanish by *ladino*-staffed literacy brigades were deeply
resented among villagers and made little headway. Following
advice from local leaders, teaching materials in late 1980 were
finally made available in English, Miskito, and Sumu, but
continued to focus on "a single, identical primer for use with
all social groups"; this uniformity was apparently "fundamen-

tal to the unifying political strategy of the campaign."[41] Since the early 1980s, Sandinista and Cuban teachers, doctors, and nurses have saturated the region. Many were assigned to more remote Indian hamlets to replace politically unreliable local educators, in many cases provoking boycotts of schools and clinics by outraged natives.

The long-term Sandinista objective was acculturation into the dominant *mestizo* culture, though various concessions to local tradition could evidently accompany the planned transition. Miskito and Creole publishing ventures and radio stations were placed under government control, and numerous restrictions were initially enforced against the use of English and Indian languages. In his November 1979 address to an ALPROMISU meeting in Puerto Cabezas, Comandante Daniel Ortega criticized Indians for using too many English words and pressed them to reject such usage and North American customs and artifacts as "imperialist."[42] To pacify the indigenous minorities who resisted creeping Hispanization, Managua has since made some concessions, albeit reluctantly, primarily in the linguistic and cultural realms. One example is the Law of Education in Native Languages. FSLN administrators calculated that political integration and indoctrination could be promoted through "national forms." Indian fears of ethnic assimilation could evidently be alleviated through the supervised revival of native folklore, language, dance, and music. In addition, with the escalating Indian and contra insurgency movement the regime has promoted several circumscribed "autonomy programs" on the Atlantic Coast to pacify local resistance, paying closer attention to Soviet methods of "solving the national question."

Political indoctrination and state control have also involved restrictions on religious freedom. Soon after gaining power, the *Frente* began replacing Moravian teachers in Miskito and Creole schools with Cuban "educators." This move sparked several antigovernment demonstrations – for instance, the violence that erupted in Bluefields in October 1980 when Creole protestors were attacked by the MPS

militia and several black leaders were jailed.[43] The demon-
stration, however, proved to be the watershed of overt public opposition among the Creoles. Afterward the regime
cracked down and banned all independent political manifes-
tations. The Moravian Church has been portrayed as play-
ing a leadership role in "counterrevolutionary activities"
and consequently experienced official persecution. This has
included the arrest, incarceration, and expulsion of pastors
who opposed government policies and the closure of chapels
and missions run by the Committee of Social Action of the
Moravian Church – at the time the sole source of organized
welfare for most indigenous communities. The remaining
clergymen experienced censorship and constant state in-
spection, and some have been co-opted to champion FSLN
projects among the congregation while helping to subdue
public disquiet.

The regime has regularly boasted about its medical and
social service achievements in minority areas after it gained
control over the Moravian welfare program. Indeed, improvements in general health care and access to elementary
education have been independently verified. Nonetheless,
some observers note that government efforts in ameliorat-
ing sanitation problems and providing medical facilities
failed to match their early promises. The authorities
seemed painfully unaware of the profound difficulties involved in transportation and construction on the Atlantic
Coast. Furthermore, accomplishments in health care have
been offset by Managua's repressive policies and the nationwide economic decline that has also depressed the living
standards of *costeños.*

Nationalization versus Native Land Rights

With an attitude common in other frontier situations, the
FSLN viewed the eastern half of Nicaragua as an almost
"empty continent," neglected, underdeveloped, and ripe for
economic exploitation. Immediately after the takeover the

government nationalized all gold and copper mines, forests, fisheries, lumbering concerns, and cattle ranches on the east coast, together with all land for which no formal titles of private ownership existed. This resulted in an extensive flight of capital with the abandonment of the region by foreign companies, Chinese merchants, and Cuban businessmen. This in turn precipitated economic decline and accentuated unemployment and impoverishment among the locals. Most Indian lands were declared government property and their exploitation subject to ministerial decisions without any clarification of native land rights issues. In northern Zelaya, for example, 7,500 square miles of Sumu territory were declared a "national reserve" and opened up to large-scale logging without any meaningful Indian input in the decision or its implementation.

Throughout the region, negotiations over land rights were persistently delayed to maximize state controls and implant pliant administrators before native claims could be evaluated, recognized, and legalized. The FSLN decided to deal directly with village representatives over land issues, so that pressures could be more easily exerted while avoiding the regional Indian organizations. Any divisions and conflicts generated between native leaders as a result of such local agreements would also benefit the regime's divide-and-rule strategy. Yet the Sandinistas met with substantial passive resistance to their schemes. Community leaders often refused to enter into any agreements without inter-village consultations or in the absence of community consensus over questions of land ownership.

State officials were authorized to set the pace of "Indian development" regardless of indigenous aspirations. According to the FSLN's "Declaration of Principles" issued in August 1981, "the Revolutionary State, representative of the popular will, is the only entity empowered to establish a national and efficient system of resource utilization." Although Indian and Creole communities were entitled to "receive a portion of the benefits to be derived from the exploitation of forestal resources in the region . . . these benefits must be invested in programs of community and municipal development in accordance with national plans."[44] Even at the formal level this policy clearly contradicted Article 210 of the Sandinistas' draft constitution, which asserted that native peoples had the right to organize their social and productive activities "according to their values, culture, and tradition."[45] The *costeños* "soon saw a horde of Hispanic cadre descending on them for developmental purposes" and implementing projects that were overseen by government agencies headquartered in the capital. To the Indians "this looked like merely another round of colonialism by foreigners, in which the Miskitos would once again take the role of wage workers and have no say in the plan of development."[46]

Socialization and Collectivization

Among the *ladino campesinos*, the Sandinistas envisaged an eventual transformation from private, family-based, and small or medium-sized capitalist farms to "socialized forms of production." With most Indian groups, however, the FSLN's "economic revolution" was intended to largely "by-pass capitalism" by changing "communal village production" into a "higher stage" of collectivization. In effect the natives were projected to become either cooperativized farmers or agrarian proletarians on state-run collectives. To launch this process, the authorities ignored or intentionally undermined the legitimacy of Indian land ownership and land use patterns – for example, the July 1981 Agrarian Reform Program, took little account of traditional land claims. All important land tracts were treated as state property to be used according to official stipulations regardless of local objectives.

To promote its integrationist and developmental plans, Managua also encouraged *ladino* peasant colonization in indigenous areas. The *Frente* reckoned that an increase in the Hispanic population and a proportional decline in native numbers would help buttress its long-term goals. Moreover, the newly settled peasants would presumably view the regime as a benefactor and protector and could act as a valuable lever for strengthening central political controls. Ironically, the colonization process was depicted by the Sandinistas as a means for "decolonizing" and "liberating" the indigenous peoples from prerevolutionary "bondage."

The rural reforms were devised to expropriate all lands considered to be underdeveloped or misused. Because Indian subsistence patterns often revolved around rotational agriculture (swiddening), Indian land use depended on maintaining access to sizable tracts with smaller parcels under cultivation in any one season. Managua unilaterally defined these areas as "surplus land" and transferred them to direct state control. Indian communities and their independent leaders viewed the procedure as simple land theft that undermined their subsistence base, economic autonomy, and territorial integrity.[47]

Prohibitions were imposed by the regime on traditional subsistence pursuits and food production techniques. Such native means of subsistence as fishing boats, hunting equipment, and livestock were confiscated to hasten local dependence on the state. Severe restrictions on freedom of movement outside the villages seriously disrupted planting, hunting, and fishing schedules. Swiddening was drastically curtailed to introduce "more ecologically sound methods" through "cooperative agricultural programs" under official supervision. In addition, the authorities tried to seal off the porous border with Honduras to control Indian migrations more effectively and guard against contra incursions. Such policies were resented by Indian groups accustomed to moving freely across the frontier and maintaining regular contacts with their kinsmen on the other side.

The strict rationing of foodstuffs and tools was imposed through a government-controlled distribution system designed to limit local support for the Indian contras and constrict village independence. The economic shortages resulting from state ineptitude have exacerbated malnutrition among Indians, with reports of regular shortages of such staples as rice, beans, and flour. Government pledges to improve living standards took a back seat to its essentially anti-subsistence policy contrived to rearrange Indian "relations of production" and enlarge native dependence on the state. This strategy was most clearly applied in the Rama areas. In early 1980 the regime suppressed the local exchange networks while imposing mandatory purchases of goods at state-run stores. Simultaneously, the authorities combated authentic Indian cooperative arrangements in field planting and other communal tasks. FSLN cadres set about determining the amount of land to be cultivated, the produce to be harvested, and the prices to be paid for all local goods and services. Bernard Nietschman summarizes the situation:

> The Sandinistas imposed control over everything Rama: Rama land was claimed by the state, Rama resources were claimed by the state, the Rama economy was dominated by the state, and as a people the Rama were to be erased—their identity exterminated, and they were to become Nicaraguan *campesinos* who worked for and supported the Sandinista Revolution.[48]

While nominally and partially preserving a "balanced" or "mixed" economy, consisting of private, cooperative, and state agriculture, the long-term direction on the Atlantic Coast, as elsewhere in Nicaragua, was geared toward "socialized forms of rural production." Unlike in the west of the country, however, the government was not reliant on Indian agriculture for essential export earnings or food staples for domestic consumption. It therefore felt less constrained in eliminating community cultivation patterns and preventing the growth of privatized agriculture. Sandinista leaders purposely sought to eradicate the kinship-based and household-centered systems of production and distribution in a society where every economic activity was conducted within a context of interpersonal rights and obligations. Economic levers thereby served as invaluable instruments of political and social control for the regime.

State farms and cooperatives have been introduced throughout the region, though their precise number and membership have been difficult to ascertain. Pressures have been exerted on Indians to join the collectives and to enlist in the appropriate mass organizations. Though outright coercion was uncommon, individuals who refused to enroll were often disallowed sufficient technical assistance, agricultural credits, or markets in which to sell their produce. To enhance native dependence on the state, the authorities also squeezed out local merchants who traditionally sold subsistence tools and other necessary items. Instead, the regime established official distribution points, including a central warehouse in each village. Henceforth, the sale, exchange, and distribution of goods was closely monitored by FSLN officials, who often denied them to people opposing government policy or refusing to join the rural cooperatives and mass organizations.

To encourage cooperative farming, the regime made credits contingent upon the cultivation of specific crops such as rice. To receive loans, the locals were often required to work on the newly formed cooperatives where they had to conform to the management's production schedules. Sandinista "agricultural specialists" determined which crops were to be cultivated near each village. Enforced monocropism in turn increased Indian reliance on credits and state purchasing agencies while undermining economic choice and diversification. All foods produced on the cooperatives were stored in government warehouses and distributed according to official regulations regarding labor inputs by individual households.[49]

To combat Indian resistance to collectivization and Sandinization, the *Frente* established CDSs in each village to keep communities in check and hired informers to report on any organized opposition in the area. The CDSs have proved less effective, however, in Indian areas than in western Nicaragua, primarily because of the close-knit nature of the native communities. CDS members were considered spies and traitors and were often scorned and ostracized by other villagers.

The Autonomy Problem

Since late 1984, the FSLN has initiated an "autonomous zones" program on the Atlantic Coast to try to temper local grievances and help neutralize the armed rebellion by creating the impression of growing Indian self-government. To court international favor, Managua has sponsored several "symposia on autonomy" to which it invites leaders of various indigenous peoples in the hemisphere and issues appropriate declarations of solidarity. The "Managua Declaration on the Rights of Indigenous and Ethnic Communities," for example, blamed the U.S. government for attempting to destroy "Nicaraguan self-determination" and for seeking to derail the "first experience of indigenous autonomy in the history of the Americas."[50] In the meantime the Sandinistas laid the foundations for *costeño* territorial "autonomy" along fairly standard Communist state patterns. An "autonomous zone" was created near Yulu in northeast Zelaya in 1987, governed by handpicked Indian leaders and the FSLN-sponsored Kisan-For-Peace organization. Several other "autonomous zones" were subsequently planned for the Indian and Creole areas. The degree of self-rule in these territories has proved very restricted, resembling the early stages in the creation of Soviet, Chinese, and Vietnamese "autonomous regions" for tribal peoples and minority nationalities.[51]

The National Autonomy Commission, chaired by Interior Minister Comandante Tomas Borge, prepared the Sandinistas' autonomy law ratified in late 1987. It reaffirmed that Nicaragua was "one indivisible nation," equated "separatism" with "racism," and outlined the tightly constrained functions of the "autonomous regional governments." Such unilaterally imposed legislation has been rejected by independent Indian groupings as a blatant form of political manipulation. Indeed, in practice the FSLN's autonomy projects amounted to little more than the granting of "cultural rights" to natives within a process of bureaucratic regionalization. Politically vetted natives were selected and placed in local government organs supervised by the *Frente's* political commissars and security officers who controlled the regional election process. These pro-regime individuals were then presented as democratically elected and popular community leaders.

The 1987 autonomy law was intended to pacify opposition while aiding the "revolutionary integration" of the Atlantic Coast. It divides eastern Nicaragua into two "autonomous regions" — *Zelaya Norte* for the Miskito region, with its "administrative seat" in Puerto Cabezas, and *Zelaya Sur* in the Creole areas, with its "administrative seat" in Bluefields. The two regional governments, however, presided over by "regional coordinators," only possessed powers of representation and consultation vis-à-vis Managua rather than real sovereignty over local policies. The administration of both "autonomous regions" is directly subordinate to the central government apparatus and is devoid of legislative and judicial powers or of any independent sources of revenue. The governing "regional councils" and their subsidiary "municipal" and "communal" organs are allowed some say over education, culture, microeconomic activities, and local police and militia operations monitored by FSLN functionaries. Large-scale development plans, finance, currency, defense, and internal security remain under the exclusive control of Managua. The *Frente's* version of regional autonomy has also been representationally broadened to include all Zelayan *costeños*, including the non-Indian and non-Creole inhabitants. Although on the surface this measure appears to be justifiably democratic, it seems principally designed to reinforce the minority status of Indians and blacks within their traditional territories. It could in future serve to reduce native representation even within the Sandinista-supervised local institutions and organizations, limit opportunities for formulating and expressing indigenous demands, and facilitate tighter central control.

In contrast to Sandinista plans, the independent indigenous organization YATAMA (the "United Nations" of *Yapti Tasba* – that is, the Sacred Motherland) has proposed the creation of an "autonomous territory" within Nicaragua after the signing of a comprehensive peace treaty with Managua. In YATAMA's plans, freely elected Indian, Creole, Garifuna, and *ladino* leaders would engage in unhindered consultations with the government to decide on crucial local issues, including land tenure, resource use, the judicial system, education, housing, religious instruction, fiscal policies, political parties, labor unions, economic development, and cultural and social services. According to this proposal, central government jurisdiction on the Atlantic Coast would revolve primarily around national defense and foreign relations.

Negotiations between YATAMA and Managua have been arranged on several occasions. Although they signify an admission by the FSLN that it has failed in fully controlling the Indian population through its own native organizations and institutions, the prime purpose of the talks for the regime is to pacify the insurgency movement. The most substantive Indian and Creole demands for meaningful self-government, autonomy, land rights, and the disbanding of Sandinista-imposed political structures have yet to be met.

5

Sandinistas and Contras

The Contras

A fuller picture of Sandinista policies toward the peasant and ethnic minority populations emerges when examining the intermittent contra war in the Nicaraguan countryside. Managua has portrayed the Sandinista-contra conflict not as an internal civil war but as essentially a struggle between "U.S. imperialism" and the Nicaraguan people over national independence, state sovereignty, and economic development. Contra leaders, troops, supporters, and sympathizers have therefore been depicted in FSLN propaganda as traitors and mercenaries, while Managua's armed forces and militia units are presented as national heroes defending society from foreign aggression. In reality, numerous anti-Sandinista groups have surfaced in the country since 1979, and several have turned to armed insurgency because of growing government repression and receding prospects for democratization.[1] For the most part, contra recruits are neither paid mercenaries nor former National Guardsmen. They are often ordinary *campesinos* and other farmers who joined the guerrilla forces voluntarily because of their opposition to FSLN policies.[2] Many have grown resentful of Sandinista agricultural reforms, human rights abuses, political and religious persecutions, enforced military conscription, and a host of other unpopular measures.

Significant contra operations commenced in March 1982, well after the government's Communist drift had become apparent. At the height of the fighting, the contra "northern front" has involved somewhere between 10,000 to 15,000 combatants operating from bases inside or close to the Honduran border. Only about 2 percent of these troops are former National Guards; these are usually local commanders with some practical combat experience. More than 10 times that number are former Sandinistas or other anti-Somoza activists of various political persuasions. The majority of contra soldiers are locally recruited from among the peasantry of Jinotega, Matagalpa, Chinandega, and other northern and central departments. The organizational structure and leadership of the contra forces have undergone several rearrangements since early 1982, when they first emerged as a viable challenge to the regime. For instance, the main northern force, the Nicaraguan Democratic Front (*Frente Democrático Nicaragüense* or FDN) became the National Opposition Union (*Unidad Nicaragüense Opositora* or UNO) in 1985 and was regrouped as the Nicaraguan Resistance (*Resistencia Nicaragüense* or RN) in early 1987.

The contra "southern front" next to the Costa Rican border in 1984 claimed about 3,000 irregulars composing the Democratic Revolutionary Alliance (*Alianza Revolucionaria Democrática* or ARDE) and led by the former high-ranking Sandinista commander Eden Pastora. Pastora's group, in league with the noncombatant social democratic party, the Nicaraguan Democratic Movement (*Movimiento Democrático Nicaragüense* or MDN), claimed to be the "genuine Sandinistas," asserting that the comandantes had actually "betrayed the revolution" by imposing a Communist dictatorship. Since the mid-1980s, ARDE has splintered, and its numbers have declined, largely as the result of insufficient funding, internal political wranglings, and repeated military failures. The majority of the southern guerrillas subsequently entered into alliance with the larger RN, though disruptive conflicts have persisted between different components of the resistance movement.

The contras have received substantial U.S. military and humanitarian aid and have benefited from significant peasant support in some regions; yet they have been unable to spark or exploit any general uprising similar to the one that toppled Somoza. This may result less from insufficient popular dissatisfaction with the regime than from Sandinista security controls, which root out opposition much more effectively than Somoza was able to do. Charges of contra military failure in capturing and holding territory and amassing larger forces display some misunderstanding of guerrilla warfare and Nicaraguan history. The FSLN itself took more than 17 years to raise about 3,000 combatants, who for most of that period neither held any "liberated areas" nor commanded any sizable popular support. Moreover, there are the difficulties involved in organizing an insurgency against a Leninist regime with large military and militia contingents, a pervasive security service apparatus, and an assortment of political and social control mechanisms (see chapter 3). The contras have undoubtedly contributed to their problems by neglecting to conduct systematic political work among the *campesinos* in their areas of operation, and the regime has denied them a foothold in any of the major towns.

The Peasantry and the Contra War

The contra war has supplied a useful alibi for the regime's economic failures, civil rights restrictions, massive military buildup, and alliances with the Soviet bloc. Under the cover of combating "counterrevolution," the *Frente* deepened its social controls in rural areas through military conscription, the elimination of dissent, and the expansion of state institutions. Indeed, militarization was considerably upgraded early in 1981 even before the government faced any serious military threats. Drawing on nearly two decades of insurgency experience, the comandantes established various ir-

regular warfare units alongside their security forces to iso-
late and liquidate the contras. The authorities also partially
"drained the sea" of real or potential contra supporters in
many war zones by relocating villagers and denying the
guerrillas reliable sources of food, shelter, and intelligence.[3]

The Sandinistas have employed economic levers to woo
the peasantry away from the rebels. *Campesinos* in disputed regions have sometimes been supplied with greater
amounts of basic consumer goods and afforded their own
land well away from the fighting, while many of their monetary debts to the government have been canceled. In some
cases the agrarian reform program has been made more
flexible in or near the war regions—for example, with the
more substantive price incentives introduced for smallholders. The FSLN has also displayed greater tolerance for
free markets in conflict zones in order to guarantee peasant
acquiescence, while land distribution and credit payments
have been made less conditional on peasant willingness to
join farming cooperatives.

Despite these tactics, the major thrust of Sandinista
"hearts and minds" counterinsurgency operations has actually aided the process of collectivization and facilitated
stricter state control. By 1985 over 32,000 peasants were
relocated from areas near the Honduran border to government-controlled settlements.[4] A major relocation program
was launched later that year; during the course of three
months, about 50,000 *campesinos* were moved from the
northern provinces to resettlement camps in the interior of
Nicaragua. By early 1987 a total of 150,000 people had been
relocated to restrict possibilities for supporting the contras
and to eliminate passive peasant resistance to official
policies.[5]

Since mid-1983 a new type of collective farm, the "production and defense cooperative," has been established in or
near the conflict areas. These Sandinista versions of the
original anti-Communist "strategic hamlets" in Malaya and
Vietnam are supposed to serve a dual purpose—that is, to
ensure defense against rebel attacks and maintain steady
agricultural output. Relocated peasants have often been

corralled onto such farms, placed under militia control, and sealed off from outside penetration and "counterrevolutionary influence."[6] About 145 of these "resettlement communities" had been formed by the end of 1987 as part of the "territorial defense system" in which cooperative farming was strongly favored. They were officially depicted as long-term, economically viable concerns irrespective of the intensity of the armed conflict. The prospect of an escalation in cooperative farming once all armed resistance is subdued cannot be discounted, but growing economic problems make it more likely that government strategy will encourage private production.

Out of a total population of about 2.5 million, approximately 300,000 people (mostly *campesinos*) escaped the country between 1979 and 1985. The most frequent accusations leveled against the regime by fleeing peasants have included restrictions on religious freedom; intimidation to join Sandinista organizations; political discrimination in the disbursement of food, goods, and medicines; compulsory military conscription; military attacks on civilians; arbitrary detention and ill treatment; forcible resettlement; growing material hardships; and damaging economic reprisals, including the confiscation of land and assets when peasants refuse to join the official cooperatives.[7] Peasants have also been caught in the crossfire between government and rebel forces and subjected to arbitrary human rights abuses by both sides.[8] Under guerrilla warfare conditions, however, which often accentuate opportunities for civil rights violations, Sandinista repression fits into a wider pattern of deliberate political remodeling and socioeconomic engineering of the rural masses.

Indigenous Groups and the Contra War

Indian and Creole armed resistance to FSLN policies has often been dismissed by Managua as a "revolution encountering temporary difficulties." The recalcitrant populations evidently remain ignorant about the benefits to be derived from "revolutionary progress." Sandinista propaganda accuses Indian guerrillas of being either "reactionaries" who wish to restore their British-sponsored monarchy, or "counterrevolutionaries" in the service of *Somocista* mercenaries and U.S. interests. Indigenous Indian and black leaders have asserted that the chief reason for armed opposition is their determination to preserve native identity, culture, and some semblance of self-determination in the face of the government onslaught. The fact that a population little disposed to rebel against the Somoza dictatorship in the 1970s only a few years later took up arms against the FSLN demonstrates the depth of hostility engendered toward the Sandinista project. Among other reasons, Indians reportedly join or support the resistance out of "sympathy for the contra cause; desire to reestablish contact with relatives who are in Honduras; fear that the Sandinistas will consider them suspect after the contras have been in their villages; and the prospect of receiving refugee assistance in Honduras."[9]

Since the early 1980s, about 5,000 Indians have joined the resistance, operating either wholly within Nicaragua or maintaining bases and supply lines inside the Honduran and Costa Rican borders. The majority established and preserved its own independent "warrior" detachments while entering into provisional alliances with the *ladino* contra forces, from which it has received some limited forms of assistance. Even according to Sandinista sympathizers, Indian insurgents have benefited from the overwhelming support of the indigenous population.[10] On the "northern front," the resistance organization MISURA (Miskito, Sumu, and Rama) was established in 1981 to harass government troops and disrupt army communications and supply lines. In September 1985 the bulk of these Indian forces were reorganized in the United Indigenous Peoples of Nicaragua's Atlantic Coast (KISAN) and placed under tighter contra supervision. On the "southern front," an insurgent MISURASATA (Miskito, Sumu, Rama, Sandinista Unity) broke with MISURA in 1982, seeking greater autonomy from the wider FSLN-contra war. In addition to these main forces, which have been predominantly Miskito-based, the Sumu and Rama have also fielded smaller combat units, usually in loose alliances with the larger insurgent contingents.

Some Creoles and *ladino costeños* also joined the Atlantic Coast resistance, particularly in the Bluefields area, often to avoid Sandinista military conscription. Attempts have been undertaken to unify the Indian and Creole movements. The YATAMA organization was established for this purpose in June 1987 under the leadership of long-time Miskito activists Brooklyn Rivera and Steadman Fagoth. It also helped improve the guerrillas' military operations. In general, however, Creole involvement in the insurgency has remained less pronounced than that of the Miskitos.[11]

Relations between the *ladino* contra forces and the Indian guerrillas have been less than smooth over the years. Attempts to maintain effective cooperation have often broken down because of differing priorities and objectives. Indian partisans have sought full military and political independence as well as more concrete guarantees from the contras about future autonomy for the indigenous peoples of Zelaya. The contra forces and their U.S. backers have on occasion been accused of endeavoring to place the Indian resistance under strict contra supervision, undermining the Miskito leadership, pressurizing "warriors" to enlist in the *ladino* anti-Sandinista opposition, and deliberately restricting arms supplies to Indian forces. The apparent objective is to nullify the political impact of the Miskito resistance and to constrain the growth of a stronger and potentially separatist Indian movement. Contra guarantees concerning Indian and Creole autonomy in a post-FSLN Nicaragua have not been forthcoming; the issue of native rights evidently does not figure highly on their political agenda.

Managua has in turn tried to exploit Miskito-contra rifts to undermine international support for both forces and to disguise its own repressive policies in the indigenous minority areas. Official disinformation campaigns have focused on real or alleged rebel human rights abuses and their supposed wanton destruction of "peoples' property." This has served to obscure and minimize the causes and scale of the rebellion, to camouflage government objectives, and to gain foreign sympathy for the regime. Indians fleeing war zones and FSLN-controlled villages, for example, or Indians actively supporting the insurgents have been described as "kidnap victims" of the contras by the Sandinista media.[12] In reality, according to the New York-based human rights group Americas Watch, Indian refugees in Honduras are there voluntarily and for the most part "support KISAN as the authentic representative of the Miskitos. Many more dislike and even hate the Sandinistas."[13]

From the outset Sandinista policies attempted to separate the Indian guerrillas from the local population through military attacks and occupations, terrorization of villages believed to be aiding the insurgents, and mass relocations from "sensitive areas." Deportations from northern border areas declared to be "free fire zones" actually preceded the onset of the "contra war." The objective was to place potentially hostile Indian communities under firmer military control. "Security concerns" and "threats to national integrity" were offered as pretexts for these policies. As skirmishes escalated with the Indian resistance in January 1982, 49 Miskito villages close to the Rio Coco were razed by the army, crops were destroyed, livestock slaughtered, and about 18,000 people forcibly transported to guarded settlements about 60 kilometers south of the Honduran border. In these "protected hamlets" restrictions were placed on Indian movements, and the displaced population was made more directly economically dependent on government agencies. Contrary to official explanations, the *Tasba Pri* ("Free Land" in Miskito) settlement program did not appear to be improvised simply to "save" Indians from war dangers. It followed a relocation feasibility study conducted by INNICA in November 1980. The premise and goal of this research were to help transform "unproductive nomads" scattered over wide stretches of countryside into productive citizens settled in more easily controllable units and working on cooperatives and state farms.

Despite official pronouncements that the forced transfer of villagers was an "error," further deportations of Indian communities from border to interior regions occurred at the end of 1982 and during 1983. They affected around 15,000 Miskitos, some of whom managed to escape to Honduras. Sandinista political manipulation of the native peoples, irrespective of the "contra war," has been aptly illustrated in the case of the Sumu. Their villages were located well south of the "emergency zone" from which the Miskitos were initially expelled. In 1982 the Nicaraguan army occupied several Sumu villages and installed a Sandinista administration, forcibly recruited Indian youths into the military, and initiated a highly propagandistic "literacy campaign." This action provoked a mass exodus of Sumu refugees to Honduras, and since 1982 the conflict has engulfed most of the Sumu regions, to which few natives have subsequently returned.[14] Garifuna communities have also been forcibly transferred from their traditional areas near Pearl Lagoon or have voluntarily joined the refugee migration. Some Garifunas have also enlisted in the anti-Sandinista resistance.

By the end of 1985 about 15,000 Miskitos were allowed to return to their native areas from *Tasba Pri*. Facing severe shortages of food, shelter, and medicines and exposed to the escalating conflict and continuing FSLN persecution, however, the majority crossed over into Honduras by early 1986. The ranks of Indian refugees swelled to approximately 35,000 people, or about one third of the total Indian population of eastern Nicaragua. The Sandinistas evidently preferred to depopulate the more inaccessible territories where rebels remained active than to try to maintain costly and precarious population controls. Since 1986 several thousand Indians have slowly crossed back into the country, not because of their support for the regime but because of undesirable conditions in Honduran refugee camps.

Although the authorities have tried to seal off the Atlantic Coast region and prevent access by nonresidents, they have gained little permanent territorial control outside the towns, resettlement camps, and military garrisons. The army's "scorched earth" policies, designed to cut off local supplies for the resistance movement, have also proved largely unsuccessful, especially as the Indian "warriors" are largely self-sufficient in food and other essential items. Moreover, Sandinista forces have often displayed ineptitude in unfamiliar and unfavorable counterinsurgency terrain. A "divide and conquer" strategy has also been pursued by Managua to split the resistance by enticing guerrilla contingents to surrender their arms or return to the villages and merge with the local militia and army units. Ad hoc cease-fire arrangements have been negotiated with local guerrilla commanders, involving offers of amnesty and pledges about an end to repression and greater political representation. The government has also tried to play on the political differences within the Indian movement and on intertribal disputes to enhance its pacification drive on the East Coast.

The Sandinistas continue to impose their own system of rule in the indigenous regions while holding largely cosmetic "consultative meetings" with Indian and Creole leaders to legitimate their decisions.[15] They have also established nominally independent Indian and Creole organizations to speak on behalf of the ethnic minorities, which in turn engage in widely publicized "peace talks" with government officials. The Organization of the Miskitos in Nicaragua (MISATAN) was formed, for example, for this purpose in July 1984 from selected loyal Indians resident in government relocation camps. Authentic Indian community and resistance leaders quickly denounced MISATAN as a mere appendage of the state. Since about 1986 Managua has initiated negotiations (mediated by the Moravian Church) with some genuine Indian representatives over the question of "regional autonomy" and cessation of armed hostilities. As a result, some exiled Indian leaders have returned to the country, and there has been an overall reduction in fighting and in the size of guerrilla units. The army's presence in the region has not correspondingly diminished, however; about 10,000 troops remain stationed in the department.

Following the Sapoa agreement of March 1988, a separate cease-fire was signed between Managua and YATAMA, heralding a truce in the Indian-Sandinista war. The durability of this truce may prove more problematic, however, without some long-term solutions to the source of the conflict, including the satisfaction of native demands for genuine territorial autonomy. Despite adjustments to the FSLN's minorities policies in recent years, discussed in the previous chapter, the prospects for authentic indigenous autonomy remain distant. Nonetheless, sufficient government concessions in the cultural and economic realms could help break the backbone of the Indian and black resistance and ensure at least passive local acceptance of Sandinista rule in the future.

Peace Plans

Sandinista-sponsored cease-fire arrangements, amnesty offers, and peace agreements with the contras have served to weaken the resistance and reduce international support for the anti-Communist insurgents. Like other Leninist regimes, the FSLN engages in such "diplomatic struggles" to pacify, neutralize, and disarm its armed and unarmed opponents, while routinely breaking its commitments to numerous international accords and their stipulations for internal democratization. These accords have resulted from various peace talks involving the Central American governments, including the Contadora process between January 1983 and June 1986, the Esquipulas peace plans of August 1987 and January 1988, the Sapoa agreement of March 1988 that followed direct talks between Sandinista and contra leaders, the Costa del Sol agreement to disband the contras signed in February 1989 by five Central American leaders, and the Tela agreement of August 1989. Throughout these negotiations, the regime has continued to make contingency preparations for some future "revolutionary offensive" against its political rivals. Under the pretext of economic emergency, external threat, internal unrest, and regional instability, in the future the FSLN could harden its stance toward political opposition and the remaining independent producers and seek to hasten its socialist transformation of Nicaraguan society.

Sandinista peace treaties and their participation in regional agreements with other Central American governments serve two major purposes. First, they are designed to disarm the contra and Indian resistance forces and to eliminate U.S. aid for the rebels, without requiring any major, verifiable political concessions by the FSLN. Second, they are intended to placate international public opinion and gain fresh infusions of foreign assistance for the beleaguered Nicaraguan economy. Indeed, with the cut-off of congressional military aid to the Nicaraguan Resistance in 1988, the contra forces have been forced to retreat to camps in Honduras or into the remoter highland and border regions. Although contra forces posed a serious challenge to the FSLN from about 1985 until 1988, their combat potential has been severely weakened since then. Many observers now conclude that because of the Sandinistas' political agility, the apprehensions of some Central American presidents, and the withdrawal of U.S. congressional support, the contras have become a largely spent force.

Although the actual material cost of the civil war remains in dispute, particularly when bearing in mind the persistent failures of FSLN economic policy, some analysts have placed it as high as 25 percent of GDP.[16] This figure does not simply pertain to war-related destruction by both protagonists but also includes the *Frente*'s enormous military and security budget, which began to rise dramatically even before the "armed counterrevolution" got off the ground. As indicated earlier, the military buildup clearly served a political as well as a security purpose for the Sandinistas. Managua has also continued to supply covert aid to Communist guerrillas in El Salvador in pursuit of its long-term hopes for a hemispheric "revolution without borders." Such support could be curtailed in the future in exchange for formal U.S. guarantees that the Sandinista regime will not be undermined. Conversely, assistance may actually be stepped up when the contras are disbanded and Managua feels less concerned about placating its neighbors, or if the Farabundo Martí National Liberation Front (FMLN) insurgents in El Salvador can present a more formidable challenge to the recently elected government.

Managua has experienced mounting pressure from its Soviet and Cuban patrons to scale down its economic aid requirements by terminating the civil war and gradually normalizing relations with the United States and other Western states. The Communist powers are unlikely to cut back drastically on their military support to the Sandinistas; yet during a time of deepening economic crisis in the USSR and the Soviet bloc, Moscow is reevaluating its material commitments to several Third World Marxist-Leninist states. It is now seeking visible improvements in their economic performance and a greater reliance on capitalist economic aid. This change would preclude the need for the kind of enormous annual Soviet subsidies that such states as Cuba and Vietnam continue to receive.

A new regional peace agreement between the five Central American leaders in February 1989 provided for the complete demobilization of the contras and urged the Sandinistas finally to initiate a process of democratization in Nicaragua. Details on any political compromise between the FSLN and its domestic democratic opposition still have to be ironed out. On the basis of past experience, however, it seems unlikely that the comandantes will relinquish their tight grasp on state institutions, the security services, the armed forces, the legal system, or other important mechanisms of political control and social manipulation. Some relaxation of official censorship and a guarded liberalization of the political process before the presidential elections, scheduled for February 1990, may be envisioned to gain international respectability and forge some new agreements with businessmen to help revive the tattered economy. Nonetheless, these measures should not be confused with full-scale or permanent democratization. The FSLN will evidently not allow elections or a tentative political pluralism to interfere with their hold on power or derail their long-term socialist agenda. On the other hand, any lasting political relaxation may signal that the "transitional period" of "class alliances" may continue for far longer than the Sandinistas initially envisaged when they seized power in Nicaragua a decade ago.

Conclusions

According to its official statements, declarations, and analyses, the Sandinista National Liberation Front embarked on a "socialist transformation" of Nicaraguan society when it captured power in July 1979. Its revolutionary intentions soon confronted major practical difficulties, however, in implementing the planned Communist agenda. First, the country was facing serious internal economic and external debt problems; a far-ranging and rapid program of nationalization and agrarian collectivization would simply have exacerbated economic decline and precipitated international isolation in the non-Communist world. Furthermore, given Nicaragua's dependence on capitalist markets and the unavailability of easy credit and reliable long-term sources of aid from the East bloc, a policy of economic isolation, such as that initiated by the People's Republic of China and Democratic Kampuchea after their respective Communist takeovers, could have proved disastrous.

Second, a program of radical socialization and mass repression might have helped to solidify regional opposition to Managua and possibly provoked more direct U.S. intervention to extinguish the Marxist-Leninist experiment. Without a dependable Communist neighbor, Nicaragua's relatively exposed geostrategic position in Central America would have left the country vulnerable to counterattack in the event of an overtly threatening posture by the FSLN. In such a scenario, Cuban and Soviet support could be neither guaranteed nor necessarily sufficient to salvage Sandinista rule. Viewed from this perspective, the *Frente's* successful promotion of Leninist takeovers elsewhere in Central America could in the long run ease pressures on Managua by further constricting U.S. influence in the hemisphere. In the short term, however, the prophesied "revolution without borders," coupled with domestic communization, simply accentuates regional hostility toward the regime and provides an important justification for international sanctions against the Sandinistas.

Instead of pursuing state socialism at breakneck speed, the Sandinistas very soon opted for a degree of pragmatism and flexibility without abandoning their eventual objectives. Indeed, they faced too many short-term problems to focus on concrete long-term plans. The ruling comandantes perceived socioeconomic transformations as a more lengthy and complex process than they first envisaged, given Nicaragua's inauspicious domestic and international conditions. Distinctions had to be drawn between acceptable tactical concessions and inadmissible strategic compromises with nonrevolutionary forces.

Managua decided to maintain its pretakeover "class alliances" with useful political groups and valuable economic classes to preempt and disarm concerted opposition, maintain sufficient economic output, and gain international legitimacy as an avowedly nationalist and democratic socialist government. The various non-Communist bodies were not permitted, however, to gain sufficient political or economic strength to threaten or dislodge the Sandinistas from power. Indeed, to ensure that the opposition would remain disorganized and largely marginalized, the FSLN captured and remodeled all crucial levers of social control, including the state apparatus, the armed forces, and the security network. Moreover, it fortified those mechanisms that could most effectively extend Sandinista influence and domination over the masses and provide a lasting basis for more rapid socialization should the need arise and circumstances become more propitious.

A discrepancy therefore emerged between the regime's Leninist political arrangement and its quasi-Communist economic program, in which the rural population figured as one of the principal objects of government policy. Antagonism soon arose between official encouragement of cooperative production on the one hand and the peasants' strong desire to own land and their passive resistance to creeping collectivization on the other hand. This antagonism accentuated the contradictions between the comparative productivity of private farming and the recurring material failings of state and cooperative agriculture. As a result, Communist ideological commitments partially succumbed to a more utilitarian approach toward land tenure outside the state farm sector. The regime's aim was to keep the countryside reasonably pacified by providing sufficient food staples to the population, while the government continued to obtain essential agro-export revenues through the relatively high yields of rural capitalists.

In the long haul, however, how much of the Sandinistas' agrarian program remains provisional and part of the often cited "transitional phase" *and* how much, as far as can be ascertained, is permanent and irreversible? The deciding factor revolves around the question of power—its distribution and its limitations. As indicated earlier, the FSLN's Nicaragua has no institutionalized checks on the powers wielded by a partisan political force that can alter its policies without legalistic constraints. Sandinista rule is not circumscribed by genuine political competition and does not depend on obtaining a popular mandate to undertake major policy decisions. In such a situation, almost all reforms, concessions, and compromises with capitalists, peasants, ethnic minorities, and other social groups are ultimately tenuous and reversible.

For the foreseeable future, the Sandinistas will seemingly continue to tolerate a "mixed economy" by allowing some leeway for a private agricultural sector while maintaining control over all major monetary instruments and the economic "commanding heights." They may even sanction the prolonged existence of the truncated and much enfeebled political opposition. Nonetheless, with or without armed or unarmed resistance, peace agreements, presidential and local elections, and restricted international pressures, the comandantes according to their own pronouncements will not release their grip on the most important political, military, and economic levers. They will therefore retain the option of accelerating the pace of political Leninization and economic socialization if they consider either domestic conditions conducive or international obstacles surmountable. Nicaragua's peasant population and its indigenous societies will thus remain subject to the arbitrary decisions of a dictatorial single-party system.

A general pattern can be discerned in developing countries when a Communist organization comes to dominate national affairs. An elitist group of intellectuals agitates for "national liberation" and "social revolution," thrusts itself forward as the ideological, political, and military vanguard of the movement for emancipation, and, upon seizing power, proceeds to construct a party-state machine to induce the "construction of socialism." Throughout this process, rural populations are galvanized first in the struggle for Communist control, and second in the process of radical socioeconomic change. Marxist-Leninist doctrine is "creatively adapted" to fit local conditions, but the basic premises of "historical development" and "scientific socialism" remain constant. Communist programs of agrarian socialization are ideologically justified as historically necessary and inevitable processes, whatever the tactical twists and turns of official policy.

The Sandinistas' programmatic flexibility and economic pragmatism have fostered some misleading interpretations about their supposed ideological sophistication and political moderation in comparison to other Third World Marxist regimes. This muddling together of means and ends results first from a misreading of Leninist praxis and second from an erroneous or inexact dichotomy between

Communist orthodoxy and pragmatism. Since its inception, Leninism has been developed and applied pragmatically, partly as a reaction to the positions of doctrinaire Marxists who proved unwilling to make short-term compromises and sacrifices in anticipation of longer-term gains. Even in Nicaragua this divergence has been evident in the early conflicts between the FSLN and the more traditionalist local Communist Party over the appropriate route to power. The history of Leninism consists of the inventive manipulation of prominent non-Communist individuals, political groupings, economic classes, and international agencies to further the creation, consolidation, and preservation of vanguard parties and socialist states. Various ploys have been used for this purpose, whether class alliances, national fronts, rectification campaigns, new economic policies, socialist renewals, or economic restructuring.

In this context, the Sandinistas have proved themselves to be good Leninists. They have adapted to difficult national conditions and maintained their hold on power even while postponing, reevaluating, or reworking some of their specific economic programs. To ensure survival, each Communist movement has needed to acclimatize itself to current economic and political surroundings while imposing its own social models. The nature of that adaptation and the pace of revolutionary change have varied over time and between states. They have ranged from the rapid communization efforts and mass repression imposed by Kampuchea's Khmer Rouge and Ethiopia's Mengistu regime to the semi-socialist "mixed economy" and selective repression characteristic of the FSLN. But what unites such movements, in terms of political control, social manipulation, and programmatic objectives, ultimately transcends the specific policies that distinguish them. Wide national differences in the mechanisms of Leninist rule and the application of socialist economic programs depend partly on internal factors (the strength of opposition, size of the party, state of the economy), partly on external factors (the security of economic aid, prospects for foreign intervention), and most critically on the perceptions and decisions of Communist leaders. Although some fear that gradualism could actually fortify the "counterrevolution," others such as the Sandinistas have calculated that rapid socialization could have the same effect. They have evidently learned some lessons from the shortcomings and mistakes of other Communist states; by avoiding all-out "class war," they sought to instigate a smoother transition toward socialism.

Whatever the strategies adopted, Marxist-Leninist organizations in the Third World are not seeking economic development and national integration per se, but a particular kind of development and integration directed by a disciplined single-party political apparatus that simultaneously constructs a centralized, state-supervised socioeconomic system. Ironically, in the midst of the Sandinistas' "transition toward socialism," several Communist regimes, particularly in Eastern Europe, have launched economic and political reforms that could almost be described as "transitions from socialism." More precisely, they are seeking to improve economic performance by incorporating market elements and oppositionist groups while simultaneously protecting themselves against social unrest and maintaining overall party control over the military and security forces. The results of this "restructuring" process – whether it will ultimately presage an evolution or revolution away from the "socialist mode of production" – remain to be seen. Meanwhile, Nicaragua's Sandinista leaders continue to grapple with their own severe economic maladies. The comandantes appear convinced that history is on their side, whatever their temporary retreats and compromises, and that they are promoting the advent of the socialist millennium. Yet they understand that the emergence of such a system may be long and arduous and that all of its features cannot be easily predicted. Hence, there is no necessary contradiction between their idealism and realism, particularly as they remain determined to preserve control over the revolutionary process and thereby decide on its eventual outcome.

Postscript

By signing the Tesoro Beach agreement in February 1989, the Sandinistas agreed to hold free and fair elections in Nicaragua. The elections have been scheduled for February 25, 1990, when voters are to select the country's president, vice-president, National Assembly, and hundreds of municipal authorities and local officials. In April 1989 the Nicaraguan National Assembly agreed to reform the electoral and media laws. The Supreme Electoral Council, which is the chief arbiter of the elections, was restructured apparently to include representatives from Nicaragua's opposition parties. Council members were handpicked by President Daniel Ortega, however, and the body has been dominated by the ruling FSLN with no representatives from the National Opposition Union (UNO). The government invited international observers to the elections, including representatives from the OAS and the UN. But local diplomats have not officially been allowed to observe the February balloting, and visas have been denied for a 20-member congressional delegation chosen by President George Bush.

In February 1989 the authorities adopted a new media law allegedly to provide equal access on state radio and television to all political parties. Yet the time allocated for non-Sandinista political campaigns has proved very restrictive. There are two television stations in the country, and both are state-owned. Channel Six, which reaches all of Nicaragua, is the prime Sandinista channel, bombarding the public with incessant pro-FSLN and anti-UNO propaganda. Channel Two, which has a limited reception beyond Managua, is shared by UNO, eight mini-parties, and the FSLN for 30 minutes a day. In other words, each opposition organization is limited to 3 minutes of air time a day. On the government-controlled radio stations, the opposition shares 45 minutes a day (2 to 3 minutes a party) on 5 of the 25 radio stations that spend the rest of the time airing pro-Sandinista views. In addition, newspapers and other media outlets are subject to censorship to determine whether the information they carry constitutes a threat to national security.

The new election law works to the Sandinistas' advantage in other areas as well. The law requires that opposition parties relinquish half of all their funds obtained from abroad to the Sandinista-controlled electoral council, while the FSLN experiences no restrictions on the use of state funds for organizing party rallies, issuing propaganda, and conducting political campaigns. During October 1989, a record 92 percent of all eligible Nicaraguan voters registered, despite reports that government troops were intimidating *campesino* voters in certain areas and limiting the number of Miskito Indian registrations to about 100 per day. The election, if indeed it takes place, could be very close. According to recent polls, support for Violeta Chamorro, widow of the slain editor of *La Prensa* and UNO's presidential candidate, is nearly neck and neck with support for Daniel Ortega. If true, the vote-counting process will be crucial. Ortega has ruled out the possibility for ballot-counting by anyone other than the Supreme Electoral Council. Moreover, on election day itself it will be difficult for observers to monitor both the voting and the counting at the 4,394 polling locations.

Despite the clear advantages the Sandinistas have given themselves in the run-up to election day, evidently the comandantes still fear an adverse electoral outcome and are taking some preventive actions. On December 10, 1989, for example, during Violeta Chamorro's speech to more than 7,500 supporters, violence broke out when Sandinista militants attacked the crowd. Several previous opposition marches and rallies were similarly disrupted. FSLN activists figured that intimidation would hurt voter turnout and support for UNO.

In a move presumably designed to aggravate tensions, the 19-month-old ceasefire with the contras was unilaterally canceled by Managua at the end of October 1989. The Nicaraguan army began offensive military operations against contra targets, purportedly in response to rebel mobilization and attacks in parts of the countryside. As in the past, an escalating contra war could be used as an excuse by the FSLN for cracking down on its political opponents.

The U.S. government has vowed to continue supplying the contras with nonlethal aid until after the balloting in an attempt to pressure the Sandinistas to hold a fair election. Furthermore, the contra leadership evidently has no immediate plans of disbanding. The Managua regime could use the contras' stance to its advantage and suspend the elections under the pretext that the contras did not abide by the most recent Central American peace agreement signed by the region's five presidents in San Jose, Costa Rica in December 1989. Suspension of the elections, however, could further undermine the Sandinistas' credibility and endanger desperately needed foreign economic assistance. Whatever the outcome, the FSLN will remain reluctant to loosen its social controls and unwilling to release its grip on power, even as economic conditions continue to deteriorate in Nicaragua.

Washington, D.C.
December 1989

Notes

Introduction

1. Consult Karl Marx, *A Contribution to the Critique of Political Economy* (London: Lawrence & Wishart, 1971).

2. For a valuable discussion of these issues, see T. B. Bottomore, "Marxism," in David L. Sills, ed., *The International Encyclopaedia of the Social Sciences*, vol. 10 (New York: Macmillan & the Free Press, 1968).

3. See, for instance, Friedrich Engels, "Socialism; Utopian and Scientific," Special Introduction to the English Edition of 1892, in Karl Marx and Friedrich Engels, *Selected Works* (Moscow: Progress Publishers, 1970), 103. For an insightful account of Engels's interpretation and use of Marx's ideas, see George Lichtheim, *Marxism: An Historical and Critical Study* (London: Routledge & Kegan Paul, 1964), 234–243.

4. According to Engels's speech at Marx's graveside on March 17, 1883, "Just as Darwin discovered the law of development of organic nature, so Marx discovered the law of development of human history." See Marx and Engels, *Selected Works*, 162–163.

5. See Lichtheim, *Marxism*. Attempts to qualify the supposedly inevitable evolution toward socialism and the materialist laws of history were condemned by Marxists as "revisionism."

6. See, for example, Robert Conquest, *The Harvest of Sor-*

row: Soviet Collectivization and the Terror Famine (Oxford: Oxford University Press, 1986).

7. See Joseph Stalin, *Dialectical and Historical Materialism*, Marxist Library, vol. 28 (New York: International Publishers, 1940).

8. V. I. Lenin, "Imperialism: The Highest Stage of Capitalism (A Popular Outline)," in *Selected Works* (New York: International Publishers, 1971), 169–269.

9. Consult V. Solodovnikov and V. Bogoslovsky, *Non-Capitalist Development: An Historical Outline* (Moscow: Progress, 1972), 59.

10. See V. I. Lenin, *Speeches at Congresses of the Communist International* (Moscow: Progress, 1972), 59.

11. See Robert Tucker, *The Marxian Revolutionary Idea* (New York: W. W. Norton, 1969), 126–127.

12. Joseph Stalin, *Foundations of Leninism* (New York: International Publishers, 1939), 41–42.

13. See Geoffrey Fairbairn, *Revolutionary Guerrilla Warfare: The Countryside Version* (London: Penguin, 1974).

14. For insights into the Marxist-Leninist theory of "noncapitalist development," see Clive Y. Thomas, "'The Non-Capitalist Path' as Theory and Practice of Decolonization and Socialist Transformation," in *Latin American Perspectives* 5, no. 2 (Spring 1978): 10–28.

15. For a useful analysis of communist agriculture, see Robert Bideleux, *Communism and Development* (London: Methuen & Co, 1985).

Chapter 1

1. For a short history of pre-FSLN Nicaragua, see Richard L. Millett, "Patria Libre," *Wilson Quarterly* 12, no. 1 (1988): 98–188.

2. For an analysis, see Arturo J. Cruz Sequira, "Somocismo and the Sandinista Revolution," in Jiri Valenta and Esperanza Duran, eds., *Conflict in Nicaragua: A Multidimensional Perspective* (Boston: Allen and Unwin, 1987), 135–154.

3. Fonseca also paid a long visit to the Soviet Union and returned with pronounced pro-Soviet views. His glowing account of conditions in the USSR culminated in the book *Un Nicara-*

güense en Moscu [A Nicaraguan in Moscow] (Managua: Publicacion de Unidad, 1958).

4. A useful summary of FSLN history can be found in Jiri Valenta and Virginia Valenta, "The FSLN in Power," in Valenta and Duran, eds., *Conflict in Nicaragua*, 6–13. For essential reading on the Sandinista seizure and consolidation of power, see Shirley Christian, *Nicaragua: Revolution in the Family* (New York: Vintage Books, 1986).

5. The first revolutionary movement to use Sandino's name was cofounded by Eden Pastora in 1959. He later joined the FSLN and fought as the famous "Commander Zero," but defected from the regime in 1982, criticizing the leaders for their totalitarian tendencies. See Eden Pastora Gomez, "A Revolution Betrayed," in Mark Falcoff and Robert Royal, eds., *Crisis and Opportunity: U.S. Policy in Central America and the Caribbean* (Washington, D.C.: Ethics and Public Policy Center, 1984), 399–405.

6. See Pilar Arias, ed., *Nicaragua: Revolución–Relatos de Combatientes del Frente Sandinista* (Mexico: Siglo Veintiuno, 1980), 85.

7. Ricardo E. Chavarria, "The Nicaraguan Insurrection: An Appraisal of Its Originality," in Thomas W. Walker, ed., *Nicaragua in Revolution* (New York: Praeger, 1982), 29.

8. See, for example, Henri Weber, *Nicaragua: The Sandinist Revolution* (London: Verso Editions, 1981). For a helpful account of the 1977–1979 insurrection and the FSLN's role, see John A. Booth, *The End and the Beginning: The Nicaraguan Revolution* (Boulder: Westview Press, 1982), 157–183. See also, Carlos M. Vilas, *The Sandinista Revolution: National Liberation and Social Transformation in Central America* (New York: Monthly Review Press, 1986), 125.

9. For a pertinent attempt to squeeze the Nicaraguan rebellion against Somoza into a Marxist-Leninist class analysis, see Orlando Nunez Soto, "The Third Force in National Liberation Movements," *Latin American Perspectives* 8, no. 2 (Spring 1981): 5–22.

10. The stress on the "third force" seems at odds with Marx's and Engels's observation: "The lower middle class, the small manufacturer, the shopkeeper, the artisan, the peasant, all these fight against the bourgeoisie to save from extinction their existence as fractions of the middle class. They are therefore not revolutionary but conservative. Nay more, they are reactionary, for they try to

roll back the wheel of history." They also acknowledged, however, that these classes could be used by Communists in the struggle for power: "If by chance they are revolutionary, they are so only in view of their impending transfer into the proletariat; they thus defend not their present but their future interests, they desert their own standpoint to place themselves at that of the proletariat." See Karl Marx and Friedrich Engels, *The Communist Manifesto* (Harmondsworth, England: Penguin, 1987), 91.

11. According to the "General Political-Military Platform of the FSLN for the Triumph of the Popular Sandinista Revolution (May 1977)," in Valenta and Duran, eds., *Conflict in Nicaragua*, 285–318.

12. For a valuable study of the FSLN's "collective ideology" since the early 1960s and its implications for Nicaragua, see David Nolan, *FSLN: The Ideology of the Sandinistas and the Nicaraguan Revolution* (Coral Gables, Florida: University of Miami, Institute of Inter-American Studies, 1984). For a less than convincing assessment of Sandinista ideology, consult Donald C. Hodges, *Intellectual Foundations of the Nicaraguan Revolution* (Austin: University of Texas, 1986).

13. The pro-Moscow PSN considered Sandino a "petty bourgeois nationalist." Valenta and Valenta describe how the Comintern hoped to exploit Sandino's campaign for Communist purposes; but Sandino eluded Moscow by severing all Comintern connections in 1930. See Valenta and Valenta, "The FSLN in Power" in Valenta and Duran, eds., *Conflict in Nicaragua*, 3–40.

14. For a full elaboration of the Sandino myth, refer to Carlos Fonseca, *Sandino, Guerrillero Proletario* (Managua, Secretaria Nacional de Propaganda y Educacion Politica del FSLN, 1980). See also Steven Palmer, "Carlos Fonseca and the Construction of Sandinismo in Nicaragua," *Latin American Research Review* 23, no. 1 (1988): 91–109.

15. Published in the official Sandinista daily *Barricada* in Managua on March 14, 1980.

16. Nolan, *FSLN*, 19.

17. The 1977 FSLN platform contains some important details on the *Frente's* views on Nicaragua's historical development and an analysis of revolutionary stages and Sandinista objectives. See Valenta and Duran, eds., *Conflict in Nicaragua*, 285–320.

18. Ibid., 301.

19. Check Paul Hollander, *Political Hospitality and Tourism: Cuba and Nicaragua* (Washington, D.C.: Cuban American National Foundation, 1986), 22.

20. For an example of such justifications that obscure FSLN goals, see Max Azicri, "A Cuban Perspective on the Nicaraguan Revolution," in Walker, ed., *Nicaragua in Revolution*, 345–373.

21. An account of the origins and development of "radical Christianity" in Nicaragua can be found in Humberto Belli, "The Church in Nicaragua: Under Attack from Within and Without," *Religion in Communist Lands* 12, no. 1 (1984): 42–54.

22. For a useful overview of these issues see Eric Hanson, "Political Ideology, Catholicism, Socialism and Capitalism," in Eric Hanson, *The Catholic Church in World Politics* (Princeton: Princeton University Press, 1987), 95–122. See also, Michael Novak, "What Do They Mean by Socialism?" in *Orbis* 30 (Fall 1986): 424.

23. For a Sandinized version of the Apostles' Creed disseminated through the "peoples' church," see *El Nuevo Diario*, January 7, 1983, Managua. The creed ends with the words: "I believe in the construction of a socialist, Marxist and Leninist society. . . . I believe in the power of the people in the hands of workers and *campesinos*, and in their existence until the end of time. Amen." The FSLN's religious campaign is comprehensively described in Humberto Belli, *Breaking Faith: The Sandinista Revolution and Its Impact on Freedom and Christian Faith in Nicaragua* (Westchester, Illinois: Crossway Books/The Puebla Institute, 1985), 137–210.

24. From the FSLN's National Directorate, *Documento de las 72 Horas*, Managua, restricted circulation pamphlet, October 1979.

25. See Nolan, *FSLN*, 62.

26. Vilas, *The Sandinista Revolution*, 241.

Chapter 2

1. See Roger Burbach and Orlando Nunez, *Fire in the Americas: Forging a Revolutionary Agenda* (London: Verso, 1987), 9. Nunez is the director of the Center for the Study of Agrarian Reform in Managua.

2. When questioned on the difference between Marxism-Len-

inism and Sandinism, Interior Minister Tomas Borge responded: "Sandinism is the actual theory applied to the reality of the country." (Quoted in *FBIS*, Latin America, August 21, 1984, p. 10.)

3. From Arce's "secret speech" to the pro-FSLN Nicaraguan Socialist Party in Managua in May 1984. This was reprinted in Douglas W. Payne, *The Democratic Mask: The Consolidation of the Sandinista Revolution* (New York: Freedom House, 1985), 90–98.

4. Vilas, *The Sandinista Revolution*, 240. For useful expositions of Sandinista policies see Marcus Bruce, ed., *Nicaragua: The Sandinista People's Revolution: Speeches by Sandinista Leaders* (New York: Pathfinder Press, 1985).

5. FSLN Comandante Victor Tirado in *Barricada* on February 11, 1985, Managua.

6. Belli, *Breaking Faith*, 22.

7. A useful summary of *Frente* tactics vis-à-vis the "bourgeois parties" can be found in Stephen M. Gorman, "Sandinista Chess: How the Left Took Control," *Caribbean Review* 10, no. 1 (1982): 15–17, 54. For a chronology of FSLN political manipulation until 1985, see Payne, *The Democratic Mask*.

8. Rodolfo Cerdas, "Nicaragua: One Step Forward, Two Steps Back," in Giuseppe Di Palma and Lawrence Whitehead, eds., *The Central American Impasse* (London: Croom Helm, 1986), 185.

9. For some details on this "loyal opposition," consult David Close, *Nicaragua: Politics, Economics and Society* (London: Pinter Publishers, 1988), 127–128.

10. Vernon V. Aspaturian, "Nicaragua Between East and West," in Valenta and Duran, eds., *Conflict in Nicaragua*, 218. For a valuable short analysis of FSLN political deception, see Douglas Payne, "The 'Mantos' of Sandinista Deception," *Strategic Review*, Spring 1985.

11. For some details on Managua's human rights abuses, see Amnesty International, *Nicaragua: The Human Rights Record* (London, March 1986).

12. See Joshua Muravchik, *Nicaragua's Slow March to Communism* (Washington, D.C.: Cuban American National Foundation, 1986).

13. Comandante Humberto Ortega, quoted in Nolan, *FSLN*, 68.

14. For details, see Michael S. Radu, "Nicaragua," in Richard F. Starr, ed., *Yearbook on International Communist Affairs, 1986:*

Parties and Revolutionary Movements (Stanford: Hoover Institution Press, 1986), 118-127.

15. See the FSLN General Political-Military Platform in Valenta and Duran, eds., *Conflict in Nicaragua*, 309.

16. For details on the election process, see Payne, *The Democratic Mask*.

17. Patricia A. Wilson, "A Comparative Evolution of Regionalization and Decentralization," in Michael E. Conroy, ed., *Nicaragua: Profiles of the Revolutionary Public Sector* (Boulder: Westview, 1987), 42.

18. Alvaro Taboada Teran, "Aspects of the Evolution of Law In Sandinista Nicaragua," in Valenta and Duran, eds., *Conflict in Nicaragua*, 68.

19. Luis Serra, "The Sandinist Mass Organizations," in Walker, ed., *Nicaragua in Revolution*, 95-113.

20. See the International Institute of Strategic Studies, *The Military Balance, 1986-1987* (London: Garden City Press, 1986), 191, 215.

21. Consult Valenta and Duran, eds., *Conflict in Nicaragua*, 359.

22. See George Black, *Triumph of the People: The Sandinista Revolution in Nicaragua* (London: Zed Press, 1985), 197.

23. See Jaime Wheelock Roman, *El Gran Desafio* (Managua: Editorial Nueva Nicaragua, 1983), 102.

24. Weber, *Nicaragua*, 90.

25. Consult Michael E. Conroy, "False Polarization? Differing Perspectives on the Economic Strategies of Post-Revolutionary Nicaragua," *Third World Quarterly* 6, no. 4 (October 1984): 993-1034.

26. See Forrest Colburn, *Post-Revolutionary Nicaragua: State, Class, and the Dilemmas of Agrarian Policy* (Berkeley: University of California Press, 1986), 12.

27. See Valenta and Duran, eds., *Conflict in Nicaragua*, 303.

28. Ibid., 337.

29. See Close, *Nicaragua*, 141.

Chapter 3

1. For a statistical breakdown of Nicaragua's rural population, see Forrest D. Colburn, "Rural Labor and the State in Post-

revolutionary Nicaragua," *Latin American Research Review* 19, no. 3 (1984): 103–117.

2. See Carmen Diana Deere and Peter Marchetti, "The Peasantry and the Development of Sandinista Agrarian Policy, 1979–1984," *Latin American Research Review* 20, no. 3 (1985): 75–109.

3. See Close, *Nicaragua*, 36–40.

4. A former leader of the "Proletarian Tendency," Wheelock studied in East Germany and published several Marxist tracts on Nicaragua's development; for example, see Jaime Wheelock Roman, *Imperialismo y Dictadura: Crisis de Una Formación Social* (Mexico: Siglo Veintiuno, 1975) and *Raices Indígenas de la Lucha Anticolonista en Nicaragua* (Mexico: Siglo Veintiuno, 1974).

5. E. V. K. Fitzgerald, "Agrarian Reform as a Model of Accumulation: The Case of Nicaragua since 1979," *The Journal of Development Studies* 22, no. 1 (October 1985): 224.

6. See the FSLN's General Political-Military Platform in Valenta and Duran, eds., *Conflict in Nicaragua*, 306. The Sandinista women's organization, the Luisa Amada Espinosa Association of Nicaraguan Women (*Asociacion de Mujeres Nicaragüenses Luisa Amada Espinosa*, AMNLAE) apparently focuses on rural females to "shift their consciousness away from a domestic to a collective role." See Black, *Triumph of the People*, 271.

7. See Teofilo Cabestrero, *Revolution for the Gospel: Testimony of Fifteen Christians in the Nicaraguan Government* (New York: Orbis Books, 1986), 54.

8. See Black, *Triumph of the People*, 225.

9. Peter E. Marchetti, "War, Popular Participation, and Transition to Socialism: The Case of Nicaragua," in Richard R. Fagen, Carmen Diana Deere and Jose Luis Caraggio, eds., *Transition and Development: Problems of Third World Socialism* (New York: Monthly Review Press, 1986), 316.

10. E. V. K. Fitzgerald, "An Evaluation of the Economic Costs to Nicaragua of U.S. Aggression: 1980–1984," in Rose J. Spalding, ed., *The Political Economy of Revolutionary Nicaragua* (Boston: Allen & Unwin, 1987), 210.

11. For a pro-FSLN study of the *Cruzada Nacional de Alfabetización*, see Jan L. Flora, John McFadden, and Ruth Warner, "The Growth of Class Struggle: The Impact of the Nicaraguan Literacy Crusade on the Political Consciousness of Young Literacy Workers," *Latin American Perspectives* 10, no. 1 (1983). See also Valerie Miller, "The Nicaraguan Literary Crusade," in Walker, ed., *Nicaragua in Revolution*, 241–258.

12. See Vilas, *The Sandinista Revolution*, 225.

13. Ibid., 175.

14. In *Barricada*, Managua, February 11, 1985.

15. See James Austin, Jonathan Fox, and Walter Kruger, "The Role of the Revolutionary State in the Nicaraguan Food System," *World Development* 13, no. 1 (1985): 20.

16. Close, *Nicaragua*, 88.

17. Black, *Triumph of the People*, 265.

18. A useful discussion of these issues can be found in David Kaimowitz, "Nicaraguan Debates on Agrarian Structure and their Implications for Agricultural Policy and the Rural Poor," *Journal of Peasant Studies* 14, no. 1 (October 1986): 100–117.

19. See Colburn, *Post-Revolutionary Nicaragua*, 77.

20. See Forrest D. Colburn and Silvio de Franco, "Privilege, Production, and Revolution: The Case of Nicaragua," *Comparative Politics* 17, no. 3 (April 1985): 277–290.

21. For a sympathetic discussion of UNAG, check Ilya A. Luciak, "Popular Democracy in the New Nicaragua: The Case of A Rural Mass Organization," *Comparative Politics* 20, no. 1 (October 1987): 35–55.

22. Colburn, *Post-Revolutionary Nicaragua*, 98.

23. Dennis Gilbert, *Sandinistas: The Party and the Revolution* (New York: Basil Blackwell, 1988), 90–91.

24. Ibid., 104.

25. Deere and Marchetti, "The Peasantry," 99.

26. Carmen Deere and Peter Marchetti, "The Worker-Peasant Alliance in the First Year of the Nicaraguan Agrarian Reform," *Latin American Perspectives* 8, no. 2 (1981): 53.

27. Joseph Collins, *Nicaragua: What Difference Could a Revolution Make? Food and Farming in the New Nicaragua* (New York: Grove Press, 1986), 65.

28. See, for example, *Barricada Internacional*, January 30, 1986.

29. Vilas, *The Sandinista Revolution*, 166–167.

30. See ibid., 167–168, for some details on the conflict between independent cooperatives and FSLN objectives.

31. Black, *Triumph of the People*, 251–252.

32. Mark A. Moberg, "From Individuals to Class: The Dynamics of Peasant Cooperatives in Revolutionary Nicaragua," *Dialectical Anthropology* 8, no. 3 (December 1983): 223.

33. Black, *Triumph of the People*, 272.

34. According to David Kaimowitz and Joseph R. Thome, "Nicaragua's Agrarian Reform: The First Year (1979-1980)," in Walker, ed., *Nicaragua in Revolution*, 230.

35. See Colburn, *Post-Revolutionary Nicaragua*, 88.

36. For a valuable discussion of these issues consult Doreen Massey, *Nicaragua: Some Urban and Regional Issues in a Society in Transition* (Milton Keynes, U.K.: Open University Press, 1987), 53-60. Despite government measures, the population of Managua has nearly doubled since 1979 and now stands at over one million inhabitants.

37. See Vilas, *The Sandinist Revolution*, 173.

38. Ibid., 167.

39. For some stark economic facts, see George Irvin, "Nicaragua: Establishing the State as the Centre of Accumulation," *Cambridge Journal of Economics*, no. 7 (1983): 125-139.

40. See Kaimowitz, "Nicaraguan Debates," 114.

41. According to Deere and Marchetti, "The Worker-Peasant Alliance," 69.

42. For example, real incomes diminished by about 18.3 percent between 1979 and 1982, while the consumption of essentials similarly declined. See Sequira, "*Somocismo* and the Sandinista Revolution," in Valenta and Duran, eds., *Conflict in Nicaragua*, 146.

43. Colburn, *Post-Revolutionary Nicaragua*, 85-102.

44. Consult Carlos M. Vilas, "Troubles Everywhere: An Economic Perspective on the Sandinista Revolution," in Spalding, ed., *The Political Economy*, 235.

45. According to my private interviews with FSLN officials in Managua in May 1989.

Chapter 4

1. Useful summaries of Indian and Creole history can be found in Charles R. Hale and Edmund T. Gordon, "*Costeño* Demography: Historical and Contemporary Demography of Nicaragua's Atlantic Coast," in CIDCA, Managua/Development Study Unit, eds., *Ethnic Groups and the Nation State* (University of Stockholm: Department of Anthropology, 1987), 7-27.

2. There are also small Indian enclaves in western Nicaragua. Since the FSLN takeover, some Indian communities have report-

edly increased demands for recognition of their distinctive identity. The majority of the Indian population on the Pacific seaboard was decimated within a few decades of the Spanish conquest in the sixteenth century. From a population estimated at over 600,000 little more than 10,000 now survive; the majority was exterminated, died from exposure to European diseases, was deported as slaves to South America, or was forcibly assimilated. See Roxanne Dunbar Ortiz, *Indians of the Americas: Human Rights and Self-Determination* (New York: Praeger, 1984), 200–202.

3. Mary W. Helms, "The Society and Its Environs," in James D. Rudolph, ed., *Nicaragua: A Country Study* (Washington, D.C.: Federal Research Division, Library of Congress, Area Handbook Series, 1987), 72.

4. Figures based on the Amnesty International report, *Nicaragua: The Human Rights Record* (London: March 1987), 7. A further 20,000 to 30,000 indigenous Miskitos are located in southeastern Honduras and a few hundred in Costa Rica.

5. A general overview of Nicaraguan Indian history can be found in Richard N. Adams, "The Sandinistas and the Indians: The 'Problem' of the Indian in Nicaragua," *Caribbean Review* 10, no. 1 (1981): 23–25, 55–56. For a more thorough anthropological study of the Miskitos, read Mary W. Helms, *Asang: Adaptations to Culture Contact in a Miskito Community* (Gainesville: University of Florida Press, 1971).

6. For some insights on the Rama, see Franklin O. Loveland, "Tapirs and Manatees: Cosmological Categories and Social Processes among Rama Indians of Eastern Nicaragua," in Mary W. Helms and Franklin O. Loveland, eds., *Frontier Adaptations in Lower Central America* (Philadelphia: Institute for the Study of Human Issues, 1976), 67–82.

7. Researchers believe that similar groups in Central America have become extinct because of their inability or unwillingness to incorporate outsiders or to adapt their subsistence patterns to foreign influences. For early observations of Nicaragua's Amerindians, see Eduard Conzemius, "Ethnological Survey of the Miskito and Sumu Indians of Honduras and Nicaragua," *Bulletin of the Bureau of American Ethnology*, no. 106 (1983), 1–191.

8. For a fascinating discussion of these issues, see Mary W. Helms, "Negro or Indian? The Changing Identity of a Frontier Population," in Ann M. Pescatello, ed., *Old Roots in New Lands:*

Historical and Anthropological Perspectives on Black Experience in the Americas (Westport, Connecticut: Greenwood Press, 1977), 157-172.

9. A synopsis of early post-contact Miskito history is available in Philip A. Dennis, "The *Costeños* and the Revolution in Nicaragua," *Journal of Inter-American Studies and World Affairs* 23, no. 3 (1981): 271-298.

10. For an evaluation of the Miskitos' middleman position, see Mary W. Helms, "The Cultural Ecology of a Colonial Tribe," *Ethnology* 8 (1969): 76-84.

11. Check Michael D. Olien, "The Miskito Kings and the Line of Succession," *Journal of Anthropological Research* 39, no. 2 (Summer 1983): 198-241.

12. See Dennis, "The *Costeños* and the Revolution."

13. For some details on the Garifuna, refer to William V. Davidson, "Black Carib (Garifuna) Habitats in Central America," in Helms and Loveland, eds., *Frontier Adaptations*, 85-94, and William V. Davidson, "The Garifuna of Pearl Lagoon: Ethnohistory of an Afro-American Enclave in Nicaragua," *Ethnohistory* 27, no. 1 (1980): 31-47.

14. Cited in *Pana Pana Newsletter* (an International Miskito, Sumo, and Rama Support Group) 1, no. 1 (Fall 1986): 2. Nothing was said in the treaty about the Sumu or Rama, and no Indian leaders participated in its formalities.

15. See, for example, Dorothy J. Cattle, "Dietary Diversity and Nutritional Security in a Coastal Miskito Village, Eastern Nicaragua," in Helms and Loveland, eds., *Frontier Adaptations*, 117-130.

16. See Bernard Nietschmann, *Between Land and Water: The Subsistence Ecology of the Miskito Indians, Eastern Nicaragua* (New York: Seminar Press, 1973), 24.

17. See Bernard Nietschmann, "Ecological Change, Inflation, and Migration in the Far Western Caribbean," *The Geographical Review* 69, no. 1: 1-24.

18. Ibid., 21.

19. One notable grievance that did not specifically concern Somoza's rule revolved around the Nicaraguan-Honduran frontier adjustments decided by the World Court in 1960. The area's Indian populations were not consulted in a ruling that moved the border south to the Rio Coco in favor of Honduras. As a consequence, about 5,000 Miskitos were relocated away from the

disputed region, thus disrupting their subsistence and trading networks.

20. See Dennis, "The *Costeños* and the Revolution," 283–284.

21. Sandinista preconceptions about native peoples are often reflected in the works of their Western sympathizers. For example, Indians are "people with no sense of direction or historical perspective" (Black, *Triumph of the People*, 241); they have the lowest "political consciousness" in Nicaragua (ibid., 306); they are untrustworthy and irresponsible for demanding self-determination in a revolutionary state (Close, *Nicaragua*, 59). For an FSLN article underscoring the comandantes' prejudices see the interview with Luis Carrion, "Ethnic Minorities and the Revolutionary Challenge," *Barricada*, May 6–7, 1981.

22. For a useful Marxist discussion of these issues, see Carlos M. Vilas, "Revolutionary Change and Multi-Ethnic Regions: The Sandinista Revolution and the Atlantic Coast," in CIDCA/Development Study Unit, eds., *Ethnic Groups*, 61–96.

23. See the paper "Recourse Procedures and Other Forms of Protection Available to Victims of Racial Discrimination," delivered by William Ramirez, military governor of the Atlantic Coast, to a United Nations Human Rights Commission meeting in Managua in December 1981.

24. Martin Diskin, "The Manipulation of Indigenous Struggles," in Thomas Walker, ed., *Reagan versus the Sandinistas: The Undeclared War on Nicaragua* (Boulder: Westview, 1987), 84.

25. For instance, see the essay by William Ramirez, "The Imperialist Threat and the Indigenous Problem in Nicaragua," in Klaudine Ohland and Robin Schneider, eds., *National Revolution and Indigenous Identity: The Conflict between Sandinists and Miskito Indians on Nicaragua's Atlantic Coast* (Copenhagen: International Working Group for Indigenous Affairs, 1984), 218–234.

26. Close, *Nicaragua*, 53.

27. Philippe Bourgois, "The Problematic of Nicaragua's Indigenous Minorities," in Walker, ed., *Nicaragua in Revolution*, 303. Bourgois has worked in the FSLN's Agrarian Reform Institute; his sentiments toward native peoples largely echo those of the Sandinista leadership.

28. For an invaluable account of escalating conflicts between the FSLN and Indian leaders, see the interview with Armstrong Wiggins in *Akwesasne Notes* 13, no. 4 (late Autumn 1981).

29. A somewhat sanitized version of Sandinista arguments against Indian autonomy can be found in Roxanne Dunbar Ortiz, "The Miskito People, Ethnicity, and the Atlantic Coast," in Judy Tazewell, ed., *The Miskito Question and the Revolution in Nicaragua* (Hampton, Virginia: Compita Publishing, Tidewater Nicaragua Project Foundation, June 1984), 8–16.

30. For example, see Roxanne Dunbar Ortiz, "The Fourth World and Indigenism: Politics of Isolation and Alternatives," *Journal of Ethnic Studies* 12, no. 1 (Spring 1984): 79–105. The author's skewed "class analysis" leaves little room for "fourth world" self-determination in a "revolutionary state." It rests on the simplistic assumption that "socialism" removes the "principal oppressive and exploitative element in relation to Indian lands and labor – the profit motive." A pamphlet written by Ortiz for Managua, entitled *El Caso Miskito* [The Miskito case], was used as a primer by Sandinista troops fighting the Indian resistance.

31. Bernard Nietschmann, "Indian Nations and the Nicaraguan State" in *Human Rights in Nicaragua under the Sandinistas: From Revolution to Repression* (Washington, D.C.: U.S. Department of State, December 1986), 190.

32. According to the FSLN document, "The Atlantic Coast and Autonomy" (Managua: Center for International Communication, April 1987), supplied by the Permanent Mission of Nicaragua to the Organization of American States, Washington, D.C., 1987.

33. This point is debated by John H. Moore, "The Miskitu National Question in Nicaragua: Background to a Misunderstanding," *Science and Society* 50, no. 2 (Summer 1986): 132–147.

34. For a valuable overview of FSLN-MISURASATA conflicts, see Michael Rediske and Robin Schneider, "National Revolution and Indigenous Identity: The Conflict Between the Sandinist Government and the Miskito Indians, 1979 to 1982," in Ohland and Schneider, eds., 1984, pp. 3–27.

35. See the Organization of American States, *Report on the Situation of Human Rights of a Segment of the Nicaraguan Population of Miskito Origin*, Washington, D.C., 1984, p. 130.

36. An informative Miskito account of FSLN policies can be found in Brooklyn Rivera, "Problems of the Indians with the Sandinist Revolution," in Ohland and Schneider, eds., 1984, pp. 203–217.

37. See Vilas, "Revolutionary Change" in CIDCA and Development Study Unit, eds., *Ethnic Groups*, 75.

38. Philippe Bourgois, "Nicaragua's Ethnic Minorities in the Revolution," in Peter Rosset and John Vandermeer, eds., *Nicaragua: Unfinished Revolution, The New Nicaragua Reader* (New York: Grove Press, 1986), 459–472. According to the author, "most of the analysis" in this piece was prepared by the Sandinistas' CIDCA director in Bluefields.

39. Black, *Triumph of the People*, 307.

40. Richard N. Adams, "The Dynamics of Societal Diversity: Notes from Nicaragua for a Sociology of Survival," *American Ethnologist* 8, no. 1 (February 1981).

41. Black, *Triumph of the People*, 315.

42. See Richard N. Adams, "The Sandinistas and the Indian: The New Indian 'Problem,'" *Caribbean Review* 10, no. 1 (Winter 1981): 55.

43. For a summation of Sandinista human rights violations against indigenous peoples, see J. B. A. Kessler, "Nicaraguan Indians Have Good Cause to Mistrust Sandinistas," and Bernard Nietschmann, "The Miskito Indians of Nicaragua: Statement before the Organization of American States, Inter-American Commission on Human Rights," *Social Justice Review* 75, nos. 1–2 (January–February 1984), and Martin Kriele, *Nicaragua: America's Bleeding Heart* (Mainz, West Germany: Hase & Koehler Verlag, Konrad Adenauer Stiftung, 1985), 74–95.

44. Point 8 of the declaration quoted in Luke Holland, "The 'Undeclared War': Indians and the Revolution in Nicaragua," in Survival International, ed., *An End to Laughter? Tribal Peoples and Economic Development* (London: Survival International, 1985), 78.

45. See Valenta and Duran, eds., *Conflict in Nicaragua*, 364.

46. Moore, "The Miskitu National Question," 142.

47. See Bernard Nietschmann, "The Indian Resistance in Nicaragua," *Akwesasne Notes* 16, no. 2 (early Spring 1984).

48. From an unpublished paper by Bernard Nietschmann, "Third-Side Geopolitics in Central America: The Miskito Revolution and the Nicaraguan Conflict" (16 pages), presented at the International Geographical Union symposium on Latin America in Barcelona, Spain, September 4, 1986.

49. For details, see the interview with Dr. Kenneth Sarapio in *Akwesasne Notes* 17, no. 3 (Summer 1985).

50. For the full text of the declaration and the FSLN's "autonomy law," see "The Atlantic Coast and Autonomy," Managua, 1987, 10–12.

51. In February 1985 Managua reportedly dispatched two trusted Sandinista Miskitos to Moscow, Leningrad, and Soviet Lithuania to study the system of "ethnic autonomy" in the USSR at first hand. See Bernard Nietschmann, "Negotiating with the Sandinistas," Department of Geography, University of California, Berkeley (June 5, 1985), p. 8.

Chapter 5

1. For an invaluable account of the origins and fortunes of various contra forces, consult Michael Radu, "The Origins and Evolution of the Nicaraguan Insurgencies, 1979–1985," *Orbis* 29, no. 4 (Winter 1986): 821–840.

2. Details on the structure and composition of the Nicaraguan resistance as of early 1986 can be found in U.S. Department of State, Bureau of Public Affairs, *Documents on the Nicaraguan Resistance: Leaders, Military Personnel, and Programs*, Special Report No. 142, March 1986.

3. The "political and economic offensive" designed to stifle peasant support for the contras is outlined in material produced by the official *Agencia Nueva* in Managua. See, for example, their document, *The Defeat of the Counterrevolution: An Overview, 1985–1987* (32 pages).

4. Vilas, *The Sandinista Revolution*, 262.

5. Puebla Institute, *CPDH Report on the Situation of Human Rights in Nicaragua* (New York, 1987), 6.

6. Vila, *The Sandinista Revolution*, 168–169.

7. Puebla Institute, *Fleeing Their Homeland: A Report on the Testimony of Nicaraguan Refugees to Conditions in their Country and the Reasons for their Flight* (New York, April 1987).

8. For valuable compilations of human rights violations by both sides in the conflict, see, among others, Nicaraguan Association for Human Rights (CPDH), *Six Months Report on Human Rights in the Nicaraguan Resistance*, San Jose, Costa Rica, July 1987; Puebla Institute, *Nicaragua, Civil Liberties, and the Central American Peace Plan*, New York, January 1988; Americas Watch, *Violations of the Laws of War by Both Sides in Nicaragua*

in 1987, New York, November 5, 1987; and Americas Watch, *Human Rights in Nicaragua, 1986*, New York, February 1987.

9. Cited in Americas Watch, *The Miskitos in Nicaragua, 1981-1984*, New York, November 1984, p. 36.

10. Check Charles R. Hale, "Institutional Struggle, Conflict, and Reconciliation: Miskitu Indians and the Nicaraguan State (1979-1985)," in CIDCA/Development Study Unit, eds., *Ethnic Groups*, 101-125.

11. For an FSLN-slanted explanation of Creole reactions, see Edmund T. Gordon, "History, Identity, Consciousness, and Revolution: Afro-Nicaraguans and the Nicaraguan Revolution," in ibid., 135-159.

12. For an eyewitness account of Indian escape from FSLN attacks, officially presented as "contra kidnappings," see Peter Ray, "Miskito Power: Back on the British Main," *Quadrant 32*, nos. 1 & 2 (January-February 1988): 27-37.

13. See Americas Watch, *With the Miskitos in Honduras*, New York, April 11, 1986, p. 18.

14. See Americas Watch, *The Sumus in Nicaragua and Honduras: An Endangered People*, New York, September 1987.

15. Consult, for example, Brooklyn Rivera, "The Indian Negotiations and Nicaragua's Conflict," in Eleanor J. Menzies, ed., *Indian War and Peace in Nicaragua* (Snoqualmie, Washington: Center for World Indigenous Studies, 1985), 11-19.

16. See Bill Gibson, "A Structural Overview of the Nicaraguan Economy," in Spalding, ed., *The Political Economy*, 15-41. Until 1986, about 12,000 people had reportedly perished in the conflict, 50,000 were wounded, and 300,000 people (mostly peasants) fled the combat zones.

Index

Agrarian reform, 42–48; capitalist reemergence and, 8; contra war and, 91; Indian land ownership and, 81; land redistribution, 44–46, 50–52; stability of, 104; stages of, 42–43

Agriculture: financing of, 44; indigenous peoples and, 82–83; military mobilization and, 40–41; Nicaraguan economy and, 58–62; pre-Sandinista, 35–37; unionization, 48–50

Alianza Para el Progreso de los Miskitos y Sumu (ALPROMISU), 72–73, 75, 78

Americas Watch, 95

Arce, Bayardo, 24

ARDE. *See* Democratic Revolutionary Alliance

Armed forces, 31–32, 39–41. *See also* Contra war

Associación de Trabajadores del Campo (ATC), 38–39

Atlantic Coast region: historical background, 64–69; *ladino* colonization of, 81–82; nationalization and, 79–81; Sandinista central control of, 74–77. *See also* Indigenous peoples

Austerity program, 60

Autonomous zones programs, 85–87

Bluefields, 64, 78, 86

Borge, Tomas, 12, 85

Bourgeoisie, 33; agricultural economy and, 35–36; alliances with, 5–6, 17

Burbach, Roger, 23

Campesinos. *See* Peasantry

Capitalist development phase, 5, 23

Caribs, 63–64, 67

Castro, Fidel, 12, 16

Catholic Church, 20, 27

CDS. *See* Comités de Defensa Sandinista

Centralization, 7; Atlantic coast and, 74–77; democratic centralism, 28, 31, 40; indigenous people and, 71

* 9 7 8 0 2 7 5 9 3 5 3 6 8 *